Wild
COUNTRY

Wild
COUNTRY

TRUE STORIES FROM THE GREAT OUTDOORS

Ken Cook

Alpharetta, GA

ISBN: 978-1-61005-612-0

10 9 8 7 6 5 4 3 2   0 6 0 4 1 5

Printed in the United States of America

⊗ This paper meets the requirements of ANSI/NISO Z39.48-1992 (Permanence of Paper)

DEDICATION

This book is dedicated to my wife, Connie, who graciously tolerated my time away to pursue these stories. And to my close friend, David Willcox (1939-2015), an expert woodsman and hunter who became a dear friend and outdoors companion. He generously shared his haunts and wisdom. I will miss him greatly.

CONTENTS

PART V: THE INHABITANTS

EPILOGUE: LAGNIAPPE

PREFACE

What you are about to read is a collection of newspaper columns written and published about people, places, and things all intricately woven into the fabric of the great outdoors. All are true and represent the yield of many interviews and time afield.

The subject matter is broad—enough so to satisfy the appetite of anyone who has ever waded a mountain stream, hiked through a stand of old-growth forests and swamps, baited a fishing hook, harvested a game bird or animal, or listened to tall tales around a campfire.

Most of all, this book reveals much about devoted outdoor enthusiasts (male and female) who populate the outdoors—everyday people who practice conservation, make game calls, train sporting dogs, and imbue their offspring with an enduring love and respect for the outdoors.

One does not have to be a hardcore outdoors person to enjoy this book, only an average person who has briefly experienced the satisfaction of gazing out of their den window into the backyard.

ACKNOWLEDGMENTS

This book would not have been possible without the contributions of friends and associates:

M. E. "Mike" Butler, my brother and mentor, who led me at a very early age into the woods and taught me about squirrel hunting, marksmanship, and gun safety.

Gary Fleming, a lifelong friend and hunting companion with whom I still share many memorable experiences out of doors.

Robert Marshak, Ron Moir, Gary Schrage, and Tim Schrage, who collectively taught me volumes about turkey hunting in Missouri.

Herb McClure, who taught me the history and lore of native turkeys in the Georgia Mountains.

Publishers of my columns: Tim and Becky Anderson of the *Fitzgerald Herald-Leader*; Eric Denty of the *Jesup Press-Sentinel*; Len Robbins, publisher of the *Clinch County News, Lanier County Advocate*, and *Atkinson County Citizen*; Alan NeSmith, regional publisher of Community Newspapers, Inc; and Robert Williams, Jr., publisher of SouthFire Newspaper Group.

My sons, Jared and Scott, who allowed me to share their highs and lows in the outdoors over the years.

My BookLogix publishing team: Jessica Parker, Daren Fowler, and Laura Kajpust, who have collectively breathed life into this book.

Part I:

OUTDOOR ENTHUSIASTS

Unforgettable
SPORTSMEN

RAY SCOTT: WHAT'S THE BASS
BOSS DOING THESE DAYS?

An outdoor writer once said Ray Scott Jr. is to bass fishing what Bear Bryant is to football. I not only agree, but would also throw in some adjectives of my own—visionary, entrepreneur, innovator, and impresario. Ray is a "big idea" guy who looks for business opportunities. When he finds one he likes, you can bet there will be a ribbon-cutting just around the corner. His entrepreneurial spirit is what earned him the national Horatio Alger Award in 2003.

Ray Scott Jr. of Montgomery, Alabama, founded Bass Anglers Sportsman Society (B.A.S.S.) in 1968; built the largest sport fishing organization in the US; originated competitive bass tournaments; and fought tirelessly for fisheries conservation. Two US presidents, Bush I and II, have befriended him, and he had a fifty-five-acre lake on his property in Pintlala, Alabama, chosen by *Outdoor Life* as the second-best bass lake in the US.

At the top of the leader board in 1986, Ray quietly sold his stake in B.A.S.S. to a small group of inside investors, but stayed on as the organization's "front man" and spiritual leader. Some years later, ESPN took a fancy to B.A.S.S., purchased the closely held company in 2001, and moved its headquarters to Celebration, Florida, near Disney World. Ray Scott walked away from the original sale carrying a "pot of gold."

So what has Ray Scott been up to since he left B.A.S.S.? Ray became interested in deer hunting, and his Lucky 7

Hunt Club put him in charge of planting its food plots. Working with a local seed dealer and Dr. Wiley Johnson at Auburn University, he began experimenting with seed mixes and seed varieties and studying deer nutrition.

The fruits of his food-plot work led to the creation of a wildlife nutritional company under the banner of the Whitetail Institute of North America, a national firm now in its twentieth year and managed by Ray's sons, Wilson and Steve. Not surprisingly, it was Ray Scott who launched the food-plot revolution that today dominates wildlife management.

His thirty-five years of building trophy bass lakes spawned the idea of Legacy Lakes, a business concept similar to golf-course design by noted golf pros. His company works with developers of residential and resort communities to design, create, and stock habitats; oversee construction; and provide ongoing lake management. His pitch is the provision of fabulous fishing waters in your own backyard.

Ray's latest venture is Ray Scott's Trophy Bass Retreat. Ray has opened his personal lakes, home, and guest accommodations to a limited number of bass anglers. The retreat offers food-fishing-lodging packages for two, starting at $875 per person. For fishermen who mainly want one fishing day in a place where presidents, fishing pros, and celebrities have boated lunker bass, the current ticket price is $550 per person.

Most fishermen don't remember that Ray Scott pioneered catch and release in tournaments, pressured boat manufacturers to install kill switches on boats, mandated life jackets, and pursued polluters with a vengeance. He also never sought publicity for hosting fishing fundraisers that netted 1.6 million dollars to build-out the Baptist church and elementary school in the tiny hamlet of Pintlala where he resides.

MEET THE GODFATHER OF
GEORGIA COON HUNTERS

Standing in his trophy room amid a multitude of gleaming, chest-high winner's trophies, plaques, banners, and other memorabilia, it was crystal clear that I was standing close to someone very special in Georgia coon-hunting history.

Neatly dressed in Dickies overalls and a khaki shirt, Paul Sheffield is a soft-spoken, modest man of seventy-six years, with piercing blue eyes and a mind as sharp as a roofing tack.

Paul was eight years old when a neighbor took him on his first coon hunt. He fell in love with the sport and remarked, "I just enjoyed hearing the dogs run and tree." A year later, Paul was given his first coon dog, who bore the name of Old Troop, a hound that further endeared Paul to coon hunting.

Many years later, after a tour of duty in the armed forces (1957–1959), Paul bought his first United Kennel Club (UKC) registered pup, a Plott breed named Sheffield Spike.

His interest in coon hunting quickly progressed from pleasure hunts to competition hunts, and in 1960, he founded the Southeast Georgia Coon Hunters Association. A year later, his club created the Georgia State Championship, which consisted of licensed competitive hunts limited to registered hounds.

For those not familiar with coon-hunting competitions, four dogs and their handlers are grouped into a "cast," and 100 points are awarded to the dog that makes the first "strike" (picks up a coon's scent trail) and 100 points go to the dog that is "first on the tree." Lower, graduated point values are awarded to dogs two through four in both of these categories. Each hunt or cast is limited to two hours.

Paul's coon-hunting career changed dramatically in 1987 with the purchase of Hardwood Dan, a three-year-old registered Treeing Walker breed. Hardwood Dan was the real thing. He won back-to-back Purina "Outstanding Coonhound Awards" in 1989 and 1990, outperforming 16,000 and 18,500 hounds, respectively. The Purina Missouri World Hunt in 1989 capped seven state championships that year. Dan took the Jim Dandy Invitational in 1991 and was in the Jim Dandy finals in 1992 when Paul withdrew Dan because of a snakebite.

It is said that the value of anything is the price someone is willing to pay for it. Hardwood Dan was no exception. A prospective buyer once offered $40,000 for Hardwood Dan. After conferring with Nell, Paul's wife of forty-eight years, Paul's response was "He ain't for sale."

After the last Jim Dandy Invitational, Hardwood Dan was put at stud for a few years. Dan passed away unexpectedly in 1993, at age eight, the victim of an injury while hunting. Dan's final resting place is not in the Alabama Coon Dog Cemetery, but at the edge of the woods next to the old clubhouse.

If you think Paul Sheffield has slowed down, think again. "My coon hunting buddy from Waycross drives over several nights a week, and we let the dogs loose," Paul said with a smile. Sheffield's time is not dominated solely by coon hunting. He is an avid deer hunter, owns thirty-five beagle rabbit dogs, and jointly owns four coonhounds with one of his friends.

A TURKEY HUNTER WHO BECAME ONE WITH THE WILDLIFE

I'm not the first outdoor writer to write about Herb McClure of Cleveland, Georgia. Since 1987, he's been featured twice in Georgia outdoor magazines, once as an expert in hunting old trophy bucks and second as an expert in native wild turkeys. Over the past fifty-four years, his chosen hunting grounds have been on public land in the Georgia mountains.

As we talked in the cozy den of his beautiful, ridge-top log home, built entirely by Herb and his wife over a thirteen-year period, deer and turkey mounts gazed down on us, all markers of his six decades as a skilled huntsman. The amazing thing about this man, now aged seventy, is that he hunted successfully at a time when neither deer nor turkey were plentiful anywhere in Georgia and the seasons, if any, were short.

Before he was allowed to carry a gun, Herb trapped fur-bearing animals as a youngster and learned their habits and behavior. His observations of turkeys taught him the importance of patience, discipline, and perseverance. From his mentors, he earned a graduate degree in scouting, hunting, and woodsmanship. "To trap and hunt them, one needs to know the wild animals as a mother knows her child," pronounced Herb.

I asked Herb if mountain turkeys were different from those I've hunted in the flatlands. Herb said mountain turkeys were always hunted hard and became far less tolerant of humans than their southern counterparts. "You

Ken Cook

don't run off a mountain turkey; they fly off to another mountain" according to Herb. Since there were turkeys in the mountains long before the arrival of released, captive birds in middle and South Georgia, it's likely mountain birds were also a purer strain of Eastern.

Between 1958 and 1966, Herb hunted in near total silence due to severe hearing loss from red measles. "I killed four turkeys after 1958 but never heard them," he explained. Herb credits a Virginia-made Leon Johenning turkey caller for his success in this period. He became so good with the Leon's caller, that fellow hunters were willing to "trade [his] calling for their listening," Herb added.

Herb's continuing desire to learn more about wildlife led him in 1968 to begin filming turkeys, a notion planted by a friend in Virginia. Using a Kodak Super 8 camera, he filmed their natural behavior in fall and spring. "To know wildlife, you should leave your gun at home and observe game; this helps you think like wildlife," Herb explained.

His most memorable hunting moment came in 2008. "I killed a gobbler in the same place that I killed my first turkey fifty years earlier," Herb told me. It was a fitting anniversary present for a mountain hunter who has few living peers.

THE STRANGE SAGA OF BRIGHT "TURKEY" THOMAS

I first learned of Turkey Thomas from Herb McClure, a well-known Georgia mountain-turkey hunter from Cleveland, Georgia, with whom I have hunted wild turkeys and who recently published a highly acclaimed book called *Native Turkeys*.

As Herb tells the story, he killed a fine gobbler one morning in the Blue Ridge Wildlife Management Area and took the bird to a nearby ranger station to check the bird in. Herb laid the tom on the steps and went inside to talk with the rangers and record his kill.

Conversation abruptly halted when a loud turkey gobble, seemingly too close for reality, boomed just outside the ranger station. Herb's first thought was his gobbler had come back to life and was escaping to his forest home.

Once outside, what met their eyes was a man dressed in casual clothing gobbling exactly like a tom turkey and dancing in circles around the dead bird. "Oh, that's just old Turkey Thomas—a part-Indian celebrating your kill," said the ranger, laughing as he did.

Several years later, Herb and I were taking a casual, preseason Saturday morning scouting drive through the WMA when we came upon a work crew repairing the road. Being neighborly, we stopped and struck up a conversation with a man sitting on the back of a lowboy trailer parked on the edge of the road.

One never knows where these polite, impromptu roadside conversations will start or end, but most certainly, they will involve the weather, the construction work underway, and hunting. At that point, no introductions had been made, but several mentions and references about turkey hunters and hunting had been broached.

All of a sudden, the man sitting on the trailer reared back, laughed loudly, and said, "Turkey Thomas was my great uncle!" Herb and I stared at each other, shook our heads in disbelief, and began firing questions at Bob Thomas. I was on fire to learn more about this man nicknamed Turkey Thomas.

According to Bob Thomas, his great-uncle, Bright "Turkey" Thomas, was gifted at birth in 1895 with three remarkable, God-given talents:

- Bright could listen to the trademark sound or song of any bird or animal, catalog it, and play it back in his natural voice as true as any high fidelity digital recording.
- Bright could change the pitch and range of his voice to sound like a female, young kid, or even a baby.
- Bright could throw his voice like a trained ventriloquist, leaving no visible evidence that a two-way conversation had not actually taken place.

Although no photographic or written record could be found of Turkey Thomas, Bob spent a couple of hours with me one Saturday morning on the porch of his mountain home regaling me with stories of this amazing man who carried the nickname of Turkey Thomas.

Bob also took me to the New Union Baptist Church Cemetery (established in 1856) to pay our respects to Turkey Thomas and his wife Maybell, who share the same headstone. Bright was born in 1895 and died in 1962. Maybell was born in 1898 and died in 1968. There is no reference to Turkey Thomas on the granite headstone.

Born in Hemp Town, a small settlement near what is now Squirrel Hunting Road in Union County, it didn't take Bright long to realize he had rare talents. Whether driven by a sense of humor, odd behavior, or the touch of a practical joker, the legend of Turkey Thomas grew and grew.

"If Bright was on the back side of the house, out of sight, he could carry on a conversation between himself and an imaginary woman that you would swear was real."

"Bright was capable of approaching two, peaceful dogs from the same litter and coaxing them only with his voice into a dog fight in a matter of minutes."

"He was once sent to a car auction in Tennessee, and by throwing fake bids into the crowd with his voice, he completely disrupted the auction and confounded the auctioneer."

"Though he was never gainfully employed, he frequently took the Greyhound bus to Blue Ridge on weekends and sold Mason shoes on a street corner. Upon boarding the bus, he would often imitate a crying baby or a cat and have all the passengers looking under their seats."

"Turkey favored an occasional drink of mountain spirits, which sometimes resulted in spats with his wife. After one of his drinking spells that ended in Turkey being ejected from the house, Turkey was seen walking up the road wearing four neckties and two sport coats (the sum of all his personal belongings) and singing, 'I'm an old wild hog with no place to root.'"

Ken Cook

"A man once asked Turkey to take him hunting and he declined. He replied that he had to meet a man to purchase a pint of 'shine, but he needed $2 to make the buy and he didn't have it. The hunter said he would buy the liquor, and then they could go hunting. When they reached the purchase location, Turkey asked the man to stay put, and he would walk down and make the transaction. The hunter heard a conversation between two men, and Turkey emerged from the woods with the pint in hand. The hunter never realized that he had been duped into paying for Turkey's own 'shine"

"He could have made a million dollars had he lived today," Bob Thomas said. "His lips never moved, and you could never be sure what would come out of his mouth"

Bright "Turkey" Thomas was eternally silenced at age sixty-seven and was found sitting upright under a mountain hardwood tree with his shotgun across his lap.

DADDY RABBIT IS HIS NAME AND
RABBITS ARE HIS GAME

Cottontails and cane cutters don't mess with Daddy Rabbit and his prize-winning pack of red beagle hounds. One misstep and rabbits end up on top of his dog box at day's end instead of returning to their "laughing places."

Daddy Rabbit, a.k.a. Aubrey Holcombe, is a phenomenon in the sport of rabbit hunting. Though he hails from Royston, Georgia (Ty Cobb's birthplace), DR is recognized from coast to coast. DR and three of his hounds (Annie Lou, King, and Squeel) are all enshrined in the American Rabbit Hunting Association (ARHA) Hall of Fame. Hound of the Year and Grand Field Champion honors have also been shared by DR's father-son dog team of Radar and Floyd.

Although DR has enjoyed every hunt since he was five, his heart lies in breeding and training great rabbit-hunting hounds. "A dead rabbit don't get me too excited, but that pack running a live rabbit is what it's all about," he said with a wink. Through careful line breeding, DR gained his reputation for producing hard hunting, brush busting, run to catch, Hall of Fame red beagles. Daddy Rabbit noted, for example, that he has five generations of beagles in his kennel.

Catching up with Daddy Rabbit took some chasing of my own. It was deer season, and we needed private land to hunt rabbits. Ben Coggins, a good friend, arranged two sites in Madison County, and our group gathered at a convenient location. Our hunt group included DR, Johnny

Ken Cook

"Doc" Estes, Ben, Joey Bennett, ten-year-old Cody Varner, and Brent Bowie. Oh, and I don't dare leave out Hambone, Heart, Dixie, Jeb, Blaze, Tony, and Jessie.

With cold dog noses poking through the slats in the metal dog-box doors, DR assembled the hunters at the back of his pickup and recited his five rules of the hunt: "Don't jump shoot a rabbit; Announce your location often by yelling, 'WHOOO'; Don't shoot my dogs; Make all the noise you can make; And have fun." With that, Daddy Rabbit opened the dog-box doors, and eight anxious beagles hit the ground.

The last visual contact I had with DR as he followed his hounds into a seemingly impenetrable three-acre thicket of briars and privet hedge was an image I won't soon forget. Dressed in Dan's brand frayed-at-the knees brown bibs, wide-brimmed orange hat, orange-tipped gauntlet gloves, and amber shooting glasses, DR cut a singular profile. An old, cut-down Stevens .410 (his gauge of choice for rabbit hunting) hung loosely from a strap on his shoulder.

With hunters stationed around the thicket, watching and waiting, the scene was nothing short of a good-natured riot. When the pack of hounds jumped a rabbit and began the chase, DR would begin yelling "Hay go, hay go, hay go," to announce the flush. Hunters responded with "Whooo." After the shot, DR would yell, "He...ooh...he...ooh" to announce the kill.

If you are lucky enough to go rabbit hunting with Daddy Rabbit and his hounds, dress for briar busting, learn the language, and loosen the trigger pull on your .410 shotgun.

JOIN ME IN A MOMENT OF SILENCE
FOR DEPARTED COMPANIONS

Over the past five decades, I have accumulated, in a loose sense, a lot of hunting and fishing buddies. Most were like beggar lice and cockleburs that involuntarily attach themselves to your clothing and shoelaces after a day afield. These "buddies" lasted only till the hunt ended and then were summarily plucked from memory. A few others evolved into lifelong friendships that withstood the test of time and many outdoor adventures.

Not long ago, just before darkness yielded its grip on daybreak, wild turkeys in the Southern Illinois woods were silent. I prefer to think they were observing a moment of silence for the passing of Roy Spotanski, an old turkey-hunting friend of mine from years past. On the other hand, it would have been more fitting for them to gobble their heads off. Roy wasn't there listening, and if he had been, one of their own would surely have fallen that particular morning.

Hometown residents both now deceased, Jimmy Gaskin and Red Walters were fishing buddies. Every Thursday afternoon in the warmer months of the year, they loaded their jon boat with gear and headed for the Ocmulgee River. They fished only as long as it took to catch a "mess of fish," and then they returned to the landing. Once on the riverbank, they cleaned and cooked their fish and ate them. Then Jimmy and Red found some shade on the riverbank and each took a short nap. As simple as this weekly outing was, it exemplifies the essence of outdoor buddies.

Ken Cook

Tom Kelly, my favorite outdoor writer, published an article in *Sporting Classics* magazine entitled "An Afternoon on the Handles." As only Kelly can tell the story, he served as a pallbearer at the funeral of his turkey-hunting friend of forty-two years, Jim Hart Andrews. The word handles in his title referred to the "handles that run along the sides of coffins that are the final containers of friends."

Kelly described his departed friend in a poignant way, "We not only worked together, the man in the box and me; we hunted together, which tends to let you look at a man's qualities from a wide variety of perspectives. If there was ever a cross word between us, or a cross purpose, for so long a period as a minute-and-half in all of those forty-two years, I cannot recall it, and I am unable to make that statement about any other human being, living or dead."

Roy was already retired when I first met him. We hunted together in Bowling Green, Missouri, every year and he grew on me like ivy, as they say. Roy was a simple man; he loved his family, made excellent wines, cooked a mean pasta dish, and loved to play poker. If you didn't know him well, you might incorrectly label Roy as stubborn and opinionated, but I found him to be a considerate person and a genuine stand-up guy.

Whether he was my turkey-hunting partner or sat next to me at the campfire, I always welcomed his company. Roy was good with his hands, and one year he presented me with a handmade wing-bone call from a wild turkey he had harvested the previous spring.

The relationship that hunting and fishing buddies share is a deep and silent one, but one distinctly marked by respect, selflessness, and abiding friendship. It is a relationship that defies description, but is nonetheless always present and visible to those who understand it.

I missed my annual trip to Missouri this year, and I deeply missed Roy's presence. You can bet, however, that I will try to call up a gobbler with the wing-bone call he made for me. I have a hunch it will get the job done.

Ken Cook

Women in the
OUTDOORS

Wild Country

STEP UP LADIES, THE OUTDOORS
IS CALLING YOU.

Men seem to be loosening their grip on the entrance gate to the outdoors, and women are showing more willingness to step inside. Whether you agree with this trend or not, it's a good thing for both genders and the outdoor industry.

The number of hunters and fishermen is tumbling significantly. Between 1996 and 2006, anglers declined 15% and hunters declined 10% (2006 National Survey of Fishing, Hunting, and Wildlife-Associated Recreation, USFWS). This downward trend has been going on for some time, and the impact on fish and wildlife populations, conservation groups, state agencies, and product manufacturers is a reduction in operating budgets.

Females represent 51% of the general population of the United States but only 2.3% of those who participate in hunting activities (2006 Northeastern Recreation Research Symposium). However, female participation in hunting has nearly doubled over the last decade due to changing attitudes and roles in society.

If your kids are getting older, maybe you've been thinking about learning more outdoor skills and participating in hunting or fishing with your husband or family. I say, GO FOR IT! Participation will increase your confidence, self-esteem, and outdoor awareness, and provide you unparalleled "quality time" with your spouse and children.

Here are two organizations I recommend to help you get started on this journey:

Becoming an Outdoors Woman (BOW). Started in 1991, this group was the first and is the oldest of the organizations catering to women's outdoor interests. BOW's half-day courses and three-day workshops are now held in forty states and five Canadian provinces. Over 200,000 women have become "outdoor women" since BOW was founded.

BOW's three-day, outdoor skills workshops are split into equal thirds among hunting/shooting, fishing, and other activities such as canoeing, camping, photography, archery, outdoor cooking, and many others. Workshop participants, who must be eighteen or over, choose four different classes to engage in over a weekend. Workshops are held at camps and resorts where food and lodging are available. The cost of a weekend workshop runs between $135 and $300, depending on the hosting location.

Peggy Farrell, Director of BOW, told me the age range of participants is thirty-four to fifty-five and about 30% of attendees come back for additional workshops. "Our instructors teach at a comfortable, non-stressful pace, and we also serve women in transition (cancer survivors, spouse loss, early retirement, etc.)," she said. "Women leave our program with greater self-image and an 'I can do it' attitude," Peggy added.

To see what courses and workshops are available, go online at www.uwsp.edu/CNR/bow/ and click on "find a workshop."

Women in the Outdoors (WIO). This women's outreach program was organized in the late 1990s and is run by the National Wild Turkey Federation (NWTF) in Edgefield, South Carolina. Teresa Carroll coordinates the program. Nationally, WIO offers over three hundred one-day events and weekend courses each year. The typical one-day event costs $50, and weekend retreats are $160+ (includes food and lodging), depending on hosting location. Approximately thirty participants sign up for each event or retreat.

Unlike BOW, Women in the Outdoors is a membership organization. When you register and pay for a WIO course, you automatically become a member and are entitled to receive a newsletter, special discounts, and other goodies. Currently, WIO has 40,000 members with an average age of thirty-eight years. Courses are open to participants fourteen years and older.

You can check out scheduled WIO events by going online at www.womenintheoutdoors.org.

If your interest is piqued, but you're still not sure you want to attend one of these courses, I would ask you to do two things: go to these two web sites and review them thoroughly; and secondly, purchase a book called *Heart Shots: Women Write About Hunting* by Mary Zeiss Stange. It's available online from Stackpole Books. Another good read is *Thrill of the Chase*, edited by Kathy Etling and Susan Reneau, from Safari Press.

HUNTRESS AND HORSEWOMAN
EXTRAORDINAIRE!

Any outdoors person would be hard-pressed (and stressed) to duplicate the remarkable achievements of Jessica Giddens, a striking young woman with a winsome smile who hails from Georgia. Her story reads like a fairy tale, but there was no wand-waving fairy godmother charting Jessica's course, only talent, hard work, clear career goals, and a supportive family.

Raised on a large farm, Jessica, the daughter of Hampton and Joan Giddens, has always been involved with livestock and horses. She worked as a veterinary assistant for twelve years and started raising and selling her own horses at age eighteen. She also earned a master's degree in Animal and Dairy Sciences

Jessica's love of horses never dimmed throughout her childhood and into college. Her packing list for the initial trip to college included a paint horse named Gucci Gunner, a horse trailer, and a late-model Chevy 4x4. Although reining is her favorite class at horse shows, Jessica has competed in almost every type of equine competition. She is a life member of the American Quarter Horse Association (AQHA) and belongs to the American Paint Horse Association (APHA).

Just in case you're wondering what horses and farm animals have to do with hunting expertise, the answer is, plenty. Skilled at archery, long guns, and muzzleloaders, Jessica started shooting on 4-H teams at age twelve and took her first whitetail buck at fifteen. "My mom was my coach on form and technique; Dad taught me about ballistics and the technical points of shooting," she said.

Jessica's hunting scorecard is exceptional. She has taken trophy-class whitetail, elk, and mule deer, and a SCI Gold Class axis deer. She also serves on the Pro Staffs of Mossy Oak, Browning, and Commando Game Calls. Her whitetail hunt appears on Mossy Oak's Mega Bucks 12 DVD.

When reality TV shows started gaining popularity around 2005, ESPN Outdoors launched its version titled *The Ultimate Outdoorsman Search*. It was a single-elimination competition that began with an outdoor essay, progressed to a video casting session, and narrowed to twelve finalists from a beginning field of 40,000 contestants. The final round involved four hunting trips: wing shooting in Georgia, a turkey hunt in South Dakota, bass fishing in Alabama, and hunting axis deer in Florida. The Ultimate Outdoorsman (or woman in this case) title went to Jessica Giddens, and she celebrated her victory on an elk hunt in Chama, New Mexico.

"Whether it's horses or game animals, domestic or wild, you are still dealing with animals and nature, and both are interwoven and connected," Jessica observed. "We are blessed with natural resources, a hunting heritage, and strong family ties that should never be undervalued," she concluded. Jessica speaks with authority and from experience, and I couldn't agree more.

THE LEE FAMILY TRADITION

An outdoor writer never really knows for sure what will greet him at the end of a dirt road, but in this case, White Tail Road led me through densely planted pines and lush, green food plots to the lovely home of the Lees. The couple and their two sons, eleven and seven, live in a rural area of South Georgia.

The Lees are a close-knit, religious family and passionate about hunting, not only as individuals, but also as a family. Each year they travel out of state in search of big game animals, and the entire family makes the trip. And they have been doing it that way since the boys were very young. Mrs. Lee once wrote in her diary, "Bigger and better things can be accomplished when a family works together as a team."

Mrs. Lee grew up in a hunting household where their hunting heritage was valued and protected. As a youngster, she went on deer and hog hunts with her father and his pack of dogs. Mr. Lee's family did not hunt, but his friends introduced him to hunting deer and turkey.

Their shared love of hunting likely drew the couple together during their engagement. On the morning of their wedding day in 1997, the couple went deer hunting.

One of the great things hunting families do is pass the heritage down to their children. The eldest son, at eleven, has already killed a bear, a hog, and two turkey gobblers. The youngest son, no doubt, will not be far behind. The Lees also practice something called "sharing the shot." If one of the family members took a bear on their last trip, another is given "first dibs" when a bear is spotted on their next outing.

Mrs. Lee has taken a remarkable number of game animals on their annual hunts:

- A Corsican ram in the Gila Mountains of New Mexico in 2014;
- A mountain lion in Utah in 2009;
- A black bear in Canada in 2000 and a second one in 2013;
- A javelina in Texas in 2001;
- Two trophy whitetail deer in Pennsylvania in 2005 and 2006;
- Alligators in Georgia in 2004, 2008, and 2012, the largest was twelve feet, six inches, and was listed in the SCI Record Book; and
- Feral hogs in Georgia, numerous, one with four-inch cutting teeth.

Planning the annual hunting trip falls on the shoulders of the man of the house, and he is apparently very good at identifying the best locations for certain species, vetting outfitters, and provisioning the firearms. Their hunting rifles are custom-made by champion shooter and gun maker John Whidden of Nashville, Georgia. Not only are Whidden's rifles works of art, but both Lees have made one-thousand-yard shots with one of them.

In a family so unified by their values and love of hunting, you would think there would be no room for philosophical differences. But Mr. Lee admits, "I like to hunt animals that fight back—like hogs, gators, and bear—and my wife likes to pursue record-book animals."

Ken Cook

Contemplating the 2014 family hunt, Mr. Lee said, "We'll probably go back to New Mexico for a bear/mountain lion combo, maybe for a Coues deer." Whatever the destination, you can bet it will be another memory-maker in the Lee family tradition.

REACHING THE HUNTER WITHIN US

T hose who follow my columns know that I am an advocate for women who take up hunting. Since the number of hunters has been in slow decline for over a decade, women and youth shape the future of hunting and the shooting sports.

In my travels, I'm always alert for stories that inspire families and serve as a springboard for women to become active in outdoor sports. Recently, I came upon such a story in a small town in Southern Georgia.

Mrs. Roberts, wife and mother of two, is a National Board Certified teacher of third graders at a nearby elementary school. She has been teaching for nineteen years and not only holds an Education Specialist degree in Education, but has also earned an accounting degree.

Attractive, intelligent, and family-centered, Mrs. Roberts would never be mistaken for a person who is now proficient with bow, muzzleloader, and rifle (.308 and .243), and who has taken game animals on two continents. She lists reading and cross-stitching as her favorite hobbies and once joked about carrying a Vera Bradley backpack to her deer stand.

Growing up as an only child in a non-hunting household located in another Georgia town, Mrs. Roberts thought hunting was bad. "I was totally a girl about hunting and never liked it," she said. "I went on outdoor trips and was always a good sport; I just didn't care for the hunting part," she added.

At a high school debate meet in 1972, she met her future husband, and her attitudes about hunting began to change.

She later married an accomplished bow hunter and, over the next five to six years, gave birth to a girl and a boy.

Mrs. Roberts' interest in hunting came about slowly. Three factors awakened and nurtured her interest in hunting and the outdoors:

- A mutual respect and tacit approval to engage individually in each other's interests and hobbies,
- Hunting and outdoor trips were always presented to her as options to accept or decline, and
- Mr. Roberts' support and encouragement, and their shared enjoyment of outdoor activities.

She showed her mettle in 1982 on a Colorado elk hunt by saddling up and riding six miles on horseback to help pack out meat. Mrs. Roberts was often the only woman on these hunts.

By the time she killed her first wild hog with a bow in 1985, Mrs. Roberts had become an experienced outdoorswoman. She participated in a two-week camping trip, a five-day bear hunt in Saskatchewan, and mastered the bow, muzzleloader, and rifle. The wild hog hunt was the turning point for her. "It was the biggest rush there ever was," she said. "I was hooked from then on," she added.

Through a friend attending a Safari Club International convention, Mr. Roberts was presented with a budget opportunity to bow hunt in New Zealand and take a ten-day African safari in 2009. His wife shouldered her CVA Apex .308 rifle in Africa and took zebra, impala, wildebeest, and bleesbok—never failing to schedule a "spa day" between each game animal.

"My wife has grit and a toughness that people don't see," Mr. Roberts told me. "These are hard trips, and you could count on her to pull her weight, never panic, and always do her part," he added. Whether hunting big game or teaching third graders, these are excellent qualities to possess.

A MODERN-DAY ANNIE OAKLEY

Whether you hunt or shoot, most people are familiar with the true story of Annie Oakley, an Ohio farm-girl who possessed a natural talent for expert marksmanship with a shotgun. As the story goes, she applied her skills to harvesting game birds that she sold to restaurants and residents in her township.

Over time, her reputation grew, as did her income. Annie applied the money she earned to support her family and pay off the family's mortgage. Her story and feats eventually caught the attention of Buffalo Bill Cody, and he hired her to perform amazing feats of marksmanship in his Wild West Show.

Quite by accident, I located a working mom in a small Georgia community whose shooting skills bore more than passing resemblance to Annie Oakley's. Mrs. Durrance did not grow up in a hunting family nor did she shoot, hunt, or own a shotgun. What she did do however was shoot two mature tom turkeys in seven days with a child's-model (smaller than a youth model) .410 pump shotgun. Experienced male turkey hunters are awestruck at Mrs. Durrance's feat. Few would consider entering the turkey woods with less than a backbreaking, eleven-pound, feather busting, 12-gauge, three-inch magnum "cannon."

There is an interesting postscript to this story, and one that is important to tell. Here is how both events unfolded. The Durrances' six-year-old granddaughter had been begging to go turkey hunting, and nothing would do but to have her grandmother sit beside her. Grandpa Durrance roosted a gobbler the evening before the hunt and set up a ground blind.

Ground fog made visibility difficult the next morning as the three hunkered down in the ground blind. Mrs. Durrance heard the gobbler sound off and moved closer to her granddaughter. The .410 was steadied for the child with the use of shooting sticks.

As the gobbler came within shooting range, Grandpa whispered, "Shoot," but the granddaughter could not force herself to squeeze the trigger. He turned to Grandma and said, "Take the gun and shoot." She honored her husband's request. And Carol's first bird was history.

Thinking that a second outing with the granddaughter (at her request) might produce different results, the trio returned to the woods the following Saturday. It was as if someone had pressed the replay button. Same scenario, same .410, and Mrs. Durrance notched her second turkey gobbler.

However serendipitous, Mrs. Durrance had taken two big gobblers in seven days—good enough to win the Women's Division of the Morris Drugs (a local pharmacy) Big Bird Contest.

I asked Mrs. Durrance how it was that a woman with no history of hunting and shooting could calmly face two different gobblers at forty yards, aim steady and straight, and dispatch both with a child's-model .410 Mossberg pump.

"In the beginning, I just wanted to be with the man I love; I got in the truck and went with him to the deer stand. Sometimes we would sit together, sometimes not, but he always let me have the first shot," Mrs. Durrance said. "Over time, it grew on me, and I began to love being in the outdoors," she added.

Ken Cook

Mr. Durrance is an unselfish hunter who seems to derive more joy out of seeing his kin be successful on their hunting trips, teaching them gun safety and shooting skills, and equipping them with firearms that they aren't afraid to shoot.

Sportsmen
GIVE BACK

A SPECIAL HUNT FOR SPECIAL KIDS

Mr. Neal met me on the highway next to a country store and led me down a rain-soaked, sandy road to the entrance of the Adams Springs Hunting Club, site of the fourth annual Rock Dowdy Memorial Hog Hunt for physically challenged kids.

I knew little of what awaited me at the clubhouse. Overcast skies and light rain had already dampened my expectations. I thought that maybe I should prepare myself for a gathering of long-faced, wheelchair-bound youngsters just trying to make it through another day. What greeted me on my arrival was a total and pleasant surprise.

The camp was a beehive filled with laughter, hog hunting, reuniting, and socializing. Volunteers were skinning out three hogs taken by the kids earlier that morning. One volunteer was frying fish to feed the group at lunch. Assisted by mentors, two kids were sighting in their rifles on the firing range. Camo-clad kids in their wheelchairs were gathered around the campfire joking and retelling their stories from the morning hunt.

We take hunting and outdoor activities for granted, but this group of fifteen kids, aged eleven to twenty-five, are rarely able to enjoy this privilege. Muscular dystrophy, cerebral palsy, spina bifida, and other birth defects have, for the most part, shut the door on them. But that is changing, thanks to parents, volunteers, community businesses, and nonprofit organizations.

Mr. McCullough is the Georgia president of Special Youth Challenged Ministries (SYC), a national organization, and they organize two hunts (hog and deer) each year for the kids. As donated funds and in-kind services permit, their goal is to help specially challenged kids take a hunting trip of their dreams.

It's easy to warm up to these kids and to witness the benefits of these outings. It's the reason Mr. Vanmunster, who originated the hunt, travels from South Florida each year to volunteer his services. Mr. Rock Dowdy, a Dodge County farmer and landowner for whom the event is named, was also converted to the cause after spending time outdoors with physically challenged kids. He personally widened doorways in the clubhouse to make it more wheelchair accessible. The fruits of his labors and commitment were cut short by an auto accident in 2007, but he is fondly remembered and honored.

The next time you walk to your stand and effortlessly harvest a deer or hog, think about the kids who yearn for that experience, but whose disabilities prevent it. All sportsmen should step-up and support programs dedicated to assisting specially challenged youth enjoy what we take for granted.

THE SOFTER SIDE OF SPORTSMEN

Once you get past the well-worn camo clothing, high-top rubber boots, Costa sunglasses, stern faces, skinner knife, and trusty rifle, there lies a man or woman with an oversized, caring heart steadfastly committed to helping special needs kids and teens enjoy the great outdoors.

Mr. Carver, an avid outdoorsman and father of four who lives in South Georgia and works as a maintenance tech at a local business, is one of them. Working a full shift, he builds tree stands afterhours and spends most weekends tending a small flock of handicapped kids, whom he refers to as "handy-able" rather than handicapped or disabled.

Carver speaks of his ministry to special needs kids in reverent terms. "I feel drawn to these kids, to see them smile, laugh, and be a part of their lives rewards me in ways that are hard to describe. I am blessed to have this opportunity," he said. Several times during our phone conversation, he had to pause to regain his composure when he described a kid's joy from their outdoor experience.

Over the past five months, Carver has been growing a South Georgia chapter of C. Mo's Kids, a nonprofit organization based in southeast Georgia and founded by Winston Barlow. C. Mo's Kids was established as a nonprofit about two years ago and now has a number of active chapters in Florida, Georgia, and Oklahoma.

After his real estate business failed during the last recession, Mr. Barlow turned a passion for helping others into an organization whose mission is to "Enrich the lives of special needs children by providing life-changing out-door experiences that are exciting, fun, and empowering in a safe and accommodating environment. Our desire is to foster self-confidence and self-reliance through the provision of outdoor adventures including hunting, fishing, and camping," he said.

Named for a loveable, fictional, southern comic charac-ter by the name of C. Mo Buck, the moniker stuck, and C. Mo's Kids became the organization's official name. Since the group was founded only a few years ago, over one hundred unpaid volunteers have conducted one hundred or more outdoor events under the company's banner. C. Mo's Kids has served mobility-impaired kids with cerebral palsy, spina bifida, and muscular dystrophy, and kids who are legally blind and terminally ill.

Mr. Barlow is a modest, soft-spoken leader with a mind crammed with good ideas and a savvy business approach to the company he founded. He keeps administrative costs low and believes in organic growth rather than aggressive fundraising tactics. "We believe that people who know what we do will find us through Facebook and word of mouth," he proudly noted.

"Though a kill is a bonus, our kids just want to be included," Barlow said. "The relationship we establish with our kids is genuine, rich and never ends as they go through life," he added. Barlow's vision for the future is to have a chapter in every state and a permanent home and "gathering place" for all C. Mo's Kids.

Ken Cook

SHARE YOUR DEER HARVEST
THIS SEASON

Almost all of the deer hunters I know harvest more deer in a season than their families can eat. Though it's low fat, tasty, and loaded with protein, venison is a red meat eaten occasionally, but not frequently, by most families of hunters.

When deer season arrives each year, hunters begin asking themselves, "What am I going to do with the leftover venison that's still in my freezer from last year?" Usually, hunters find a way to reduce or eliminate their frozen inventory by giving it away to neighbors, friends, work associates, or other hunters.

The next time you take your finger off the trigger when a fat, mature, shoot-able doe deer walks by your stand, think about these statistics: more than 700,000 children in Georgia are at risk of hunger and are not getting the food they need to lead healthy, active lives. More than 25% of Georgia children live in poverty, and more than 870,000 Georgia students participated in the free or reduced-price lunch program.

Hunger also affects more than children. The unemployed, underemployed, seniors, homeless, and the "working poor" are all worried about where their next meal will come from. It's shameful that this situation should exist in any state.

So what can Georgia deer hunters do to reduce the hunger problem? First, get familiar with Georgia Hunters for the Hungry (GHFH) by going to www.gwf.org. This program is sponsored by the Georgia Wildlife Federation and, since its founding in 1993, has been responsible for contributing one million meals for hungry people in Georgia.

Secondly, drop off a field-dressed deer to one of the participating processors (the list is on the website and will also appear in *Georgia Outdoor News*. The processor will process the deer and package, wrap, label, and freeze the animal. GHFH will pay the processor for his labors, and he will distribute the meat to a Georgia Food Bank or to local food kitchens if they exist.

If hunters have leftover, processed deer in their freezers, these cuts can also be dropped off at a participating processor. This option is called "Drop Back a Pack."

Be aware that a participating processor (there are now about twelve in the state) may be located some miles from your home and may require some driving. Call the processor and confirm his hours of operation. Consider this inconvenience a part of your charitable contribution to the program.

Georgia Hunters for the Hungry is an organization worthy of your participation. Yes, it takes some effort and commitment, but the benefits are immeasurable. Smiling faces and full tummies are what it's all about.

Ken Cook

Sporting
DOGS

FOLLOWING MOSES

Small dogs have always occupied a special place in the Griswold household. Their names—Rudy, Oscar, Bambi, and Moses—roll off Jimmy's tongue as easily as the names of his grandchildren. Though Rudy and Oscar have now passed on, Bambi, an "apple-head" Chihuahua (nicknamed for the shape of its head), and Moses, a six-year-old Dachshund, both maintain high positions on the Griswolds' pet organization chart.

Moses, however, has a special talent, and Jimmy discovered it several years ago. The Dachshund is a German breed trained to hunt badgers, a ferocious animal loathed in its native country. When pursued, a badger will race to its underground burrow and enter it on its back, positioning its vicious claws to defend itself from a determined attacker.

The fearless Dachshund will follow the badger into his underground burrow, sinking its teeth into the animal's skin and applying a death grip. The hunter, meanwhile, will grab the dog's tail (which is double-jointed) and pull both dog and badger from the burrow in one swift motion.

One day, Jimmy introduced Moses to one of the many grey squirrels that nest, feed, and play in the Griswolds' compact, fenced, and wooded backyard. Although Jimmy learned to hunt squirrels as a youngster with his father, Moses quickly concluded that he and Jimmy could work as partners in this newfound recreational activity of hunting backyard squirrels.

Moses has developed a modus operandi for each hunt. His squirrel observation point is inside a clear-view storm door leading to the outside of the house. From here, Moses has a hunter's view of any squirrel that dares to reveal himself. When Moses makes visual contact, he turns and scampers to find Jimmy.

Another visual queue that it's time to hunt is the presence of Jimmy's air rifle next to the storm door. If the air gun is not resting there, Moses knows that Jimmy has not made preparations to hunt squirrels, so he might as well forget about chasing squirrels and busy himself with some other canine activity.

It's Katy-bar-the-door if Moses spots a squirrel and barks, and Jimmy heads for his air rifle. Moses shifts into overdrive and begins working the boundaries of the backyard like a humming bird seeking sugar water. To relieve an old back injury, Jimmy takes a seat on one of the five-gallon buckets he keeps in the backyard and lets Moses do his thing.

When Moses is hunting, this hyper-energetic little dog never stops sniffing for squirrel scent, occasionally stopping to look up into the live oak branches for squirrels that might have flattened themselves on a branch or tree trunk to avoid detection. Moses remembers and checks each location where a squirrel has eluded him in the past. Jimmy says Moses will maintain this pace all day long, as long as Jimmy remains in the backyard.

Jimmy left me with a little humorous quote of unknown origin. "I wasn't born with any money, and I still have most of it left." Yes, I thought, but Jimmy has Moses and he is priceless.

OH, THOSE LLEWELLIN SETTERS!

Not long ago, a sporting dog expert writing in a popular southern magazine named the five best gun-dog breeds in the country. The breeds he listed were British labrador, Llewellin setter, Boykin spaniel, German shorthair pointer, and Elhew English pointer.

I have hunted upland game birds behind four of the five breeds and once owned a Boykin spaniel, but the Llewellin breed and its famous breeder, Deane Harris, were a complete mystery as we began a quail hunt under cool temperatures, breezy winds, and overcast skies.

Over the course of a two-hour hunt, I marveled at two keenly intelligent Llewellins that quartered close to walking hunters, found and pointed small coveys and singles, honored points, responded well to commands, and, otherwise, did everything they were asked to do. Then and there, I decided to meet and talk with Deane Harris, a highly regarded breeder and trainer of Llewellins

One example of the Llewellins' natural hunting ability came during our quail hunt. The dog that backed our dog on point did so in a fashion that physically prompted most of the flushing birds toward an open broomsedge field rather than thick cover. Nice touch if your bird dog can do it.

In an arranged meeting some months later, Harris told me a story of one of his Llewellin protégés, owned by a devoted pheasant hunter in the Midwest. When his dog pointed a bird, the dog would break point, circle the running pheasant, and await the rooster's arrival further down the crop row. The owner thought the dog needed

Ken Cook

refresher training. Harris described it as smart, natural hunting ability.

At eighty-three, Deane Harris is a genteel, soft-spoken man who looks fifteen years younger and has the aplomb of a politician. He has written a book on training Llewellins and was one of nine national Llewellin breeders who founded the North American Llewellin Breeders Association in 2001. This small conclave shares an unwavering commitment to well-defined breeding standards and DNA testing in order to protect the purity of the Llewellin setter breed.

In 1963, Harris began his Llewellin breeding program utilizing three of the five legacy bloodlines—Blizzard, Bondhu, and Wind'em. Using selective breeding techniques among these lines, he created a proprietary bloodline that Harris christened, "Dancer." His understanding of each bloodline's hunting and personality traits allows Harris to adeptly match a puppy to an owner's specifications and desires.

After my meeting with Deane, I talked briefly with an upland bird shooter in Northeast Florida who was "taking delivery" of his first Llewellin, a six-month-old puppy who performed flawlessly in the fields that morning. The hunter's wife had already accepted the new puppy into their home as a family pet. Her husband had too, but for somewhat different purposes.

THERE IS SOMETHING SPECIAL ABOUT SPORTING DOGS

Third Place in Newspaper Writing,
Georgia Outdoor Writers Association, 2015

Over the course of six decades afield, sporting dogs have occupied a significant role in my hunting life. Gun-dog breeds I have so willingly followed and lovingly watched have included Boykins, pointers, setters, labs, Springers, Brittanies, shorthairs, wirehaired Griffons, German Drahtharrs, and Vizslas.

And, though they fall in a different breed category, I would be remiss to omit coonhounds, deer and hog dogs, rabbit dogs, and squirrel dogs. Universally, it is a mesmerizing experience to watch these dogs at work, driven by instinct, training, a desire to please, and an ultra-keen sense of smell.

According to the American Kennel Club (AKC), there are about seventy million dogs of all kinds in the US, housed in 36.5% of the nation's households. The number of dogs has dropped off some (dropping 2.8 million) in the past few years. The census takers don't seem to know what percentage of all pet dogs are sporting breeds, but the AKC does recognize twenty-eight different breeds of sporting dogs.

Never for a minute think that a hunter doesn't worship his favorite hunting dog and consider it an extension of himself and, often, his immediate family. "My favorite hunting dog" stories abound in current and out-of-print hunting books and magazines. I've even penned one that appeared as a chapter in "A Gentleman's Fireside Diary," published by *Doubles & Dogs* magazine.

Ken Cook

Key Underwood of Tuscumbia, Alabama, was an avid coon hunter, and his favorite dog was named Troop. After Troop died, Key established a coon-dog cemetery in 1937 to honor old Troop. Over the succeeding years, 185 illustrious coon dogs have met the acceptance requirements to join Troop in his final resting place in Alabama's Coon Dog Cemetery.

Henry Berol, a millionaire industrialist from New York (Eagle and Berol brand writing instruments), loved quail hunting and sporting dogs so much that he purchased 8,100 acres of land near Waynesboro, Georgia, and christened it Di-Lane Plantation after his two daughters.

At that time, quail hunting was at its peak in Georgia, and the state correctly took possession of the theme line, "Bird Dog Capital of the World." Berol started field trials in the 1950s, and Di-Lane eventually became the recognized location for the National Bird Dog Field Trials and the site of Georgia's Bird Dog Cemetery.

Now owned and managed by the Georgia Department of Natural Resources as a public wildlife area, Di-Lane and its seventy plus bird dog gravesites under spreading oaks will forever pay tribute to bobwhites and the sporting dogs that pursued them.

I, too, have a sporting dog story, and I get misty-eyed just writing about her. Cancer took her almost five years ago, but not before she unselfishly gave me fourteen glorious years of hunting highs and unparalleled companionship. Her name was Pawley, and she was a liver-colored, curly-coated, yellow-eyed Boykin spaniel, a South Carolina breed and that state's official state dog. She was peerless at pointing, flushing, and retrieving, and always excelled at exceeding my expectations in the field.

To assuage their grief, dog owners are always told to "buy another when you lose one," but I have never come to grips with replacing Pawley when my heart and mind remind me that Pawley was peerless.

Ken Cook

Part II:

THE OUTDOOR STAGE

Wild Country

Swamps and
DARK PLACES

THE OKEFENOKEE HAS MANY FACES

Darkness and daylight were changing shifts when I pulled out of the driveway of the Helmstead Bed and Breakfast in Homerville and headed south to Fargo and Stephen Foster State Park. The air was heavy with moisture, and occasional patches of ground fog kept my windshield wipers working overtime. I was in the land of pine trees, blueberries, and honey, and en route to an indescribable natural wonder known as the Okefenokee Swamp.

"I was born one hundred years too late," Mr. Johnson said, as we did a walkabout on Billy's Island. "I wish I could have been around to see what the swamp looked like and talked with the early settlers," he added. Except for a short stint as a ranger at Ocmulgee State Park near McRae, the Okefenokee has been his Siamese twin since birth.

I'd wager that few people know the swamp and its many faces as well as my guide. Hired as a seasonal worker at Stephen Foster State Park at age fifteen, he spent many years as an interpretive naturalist taking groups on tours through the swamp. He learned from them, and they learned from him. In the course of our four-hour canoe trip, he regaled me with folklore, facts, and history. Never once did I ask him a question that he could not answer and then embellish.

Mr. Johnson pointed out endangered wood storks, a red-cockaded woodpecker, blue herons, white ibises, and a male prothonotary warbler that was searching for a bonnet worm in the stem of a lily pad. I took pictures of a stunning white water lily in bloom and a yellow Spadderdock lily about to open its petals. We casually searched for a never wet plant and resurrection fern, but failed to find them. I had hoped to hear the alligators bellowing during their mating season, but I was a week late. I settled for two fighting male gators, snout to snout, whose bodies rose almost completely out of the dark water in combat.

Billy's Island is a historical treasure. Named for a Seminole chief and originally homesteaded by the Lee family in the mid-1800s, it became the location of the Hebard Cypress Company's sawmill and home to six to eight hundred residents between 1908 and 1926. Remnants of a narrow gauge railway bed and prehistoric Indian mounds are still visible.

I wanted to commemorate my visit with a keepsake, something unique to the Okefenokee, to hang on my den wall. I knew Mr. Johnson had a solution. I ordered a boat paddle from him made from "deadhead cypress," cut one hundred years ago to make rails for the lumber tram. Inlaid in this paddle blade is a bony section from an Okefenokee alligator.

In any direction you look, the Okefenokee is a continuous canvas of original art painted by Mother Nature. Whether you're a hunter, fisherman, birder, camper, naturalist, or regional historian, there is something in this rare gem for each of you.

THE MAGIC OF THE OKEFENOKEE

Over the years writing for newspapers about the outdoors, I have met, interviewed, and written about three men whose lives were inextricably connected to the Okefenokee Swamp. After talking with Ray Cason, the question struck me like a lightning bolt—what is it about the Okefenokee that takes hold of people, holds them forever captive, and refuses to let them loose?

Before his retirement in 1977 as a law enforcement officer for the US Fish and Wildlife Service, Barney Cone (now deceased) spent twenty-seven years in the Swamp apprehending gator poachers, moonshiners, and wildlife violators He cloaked his stories in a blend of humor, but also swatches of reverence and fondness.

Marty Johnson became a self-made interpretive naturalist and historian on the Okefenokee. He guides visitors on canoe trips into the swamp and feeds their imagination with the sights, sounds, and folklore that are uniquely Okefenokee.

Ray Cason, is a relatively young and energetic man of forty whose grandfather and father introduced him to the Okefenokee as a youngster. He soon became an expert Okefenokee angler. Ray fishes at every opportunity and the swamp is always his destination.

You may not quickly recognize the phrase, but the whole world knows about the "alligator feeding frenzy" Ray videotaped a couple of years ago near the boat basin at Stephen Foster State Park. The footage went viral on the Internet and was viewed around the world.

What was not so obvious about the phenomenon was that Ray, a naturalist at heart, was carrying a video camera and shot footage for forty-five minutes from his jon boat in the middle of hundreds of writhing gators. "If I had fallen in that mass, all they would have found would have been my shoestrings," Ray commented.

Though never before recorded or verbally told, Ray reasoned that two groups of alligators had a plan and were working together, herding baitfish to a pinch point where they were easier prey for the carnivores. "Every time I go down there, I see something different. You never know what you'll see behind the next tree, and it's the most beautiful, interesting place in the world; it's my escape," Ray added.

These three men are but a small number of area residents for whom the Okefenokee is a magic elixir, drawing them past the portals of the swamp, again and again, to be surprised, informed, and entertained by natural phenomena seen nowhere else.

I have only been in the Okefenokee three times, but I was hypnotized by once-in-a lifetime observations that, like the Sirens of Greek mythology, keep calling me back. The Okefenokee is an alluring place with its own natural magnetic pull.

THE OLD MAN AND THE SWAMP

I n the early morning hours of June 6, 1944, William C. "Barney" Cone of Fargo, Georgia, dutifully took his place among the assault troops making their way toward Omaha Beach on the rugged Normandy coast.

The sky was filled with a torrent of bullets from machine guns, mortars, and small artillery. Though the US forces eventually prevailed, several thousand soldiers lost their lives in the bloodiest of the D-Day amphibious landings. It was not Barney Cone's time to go. Before WWII ended, he was awarded the Bronze Star, Purple Heart, and Good Conduct Medal.

Battle tested and tempered, Barney (deceased in 2014) returned to Fargo, where, for the ensuing sixty-seven years, he has confronted and conquered many other challenges in his life, some fully capable of taking him from our midst.

At ninety-three, Barney was a small man with a quiet and courteous demeanor. He spoke softly and had a wry sense of humor. When faced with a question, he would pause before responding. Barney could recall dates, names, and places as crisply as fishing line spooling off a bait-casting reel. He was a remarkable man—not only because of his age, but also because of the way he has lived his life, including sixty-nine years of marriage to his wife, Louise.

Barney grew up in and around the Okefenokee Swamp, years before it became a National Wildlife Refuge in 1936. During the depression years, at age fifteen, he worked for the Civilian Conservation Corps (CCC). After the war, Barney was employed by Superior Pine in Fargo and the St.

Regis paper company. In 1950, he joined the US Fish and Wildlife Service as a law enforcement officer assigned to the refuge, where he remained until his retirement in 1977.

For decades, alligator poaching was a lucrative and widespread criminal activity in the refuge. Hides were bringing $1 per foot, and poachers were coming from as far away as Texas and New York State during the lean depression years. Barney told the story of one of his earlier collars who was tried in Savannah, found guilty by the judge, and given a healthy fine. After the sentence was read, the poacher tauntingly said, "I'll make this fine up tonight." Sure enough, Barney caught him poaching that night and arrested him a second time.

Once when trying to corner and arrest a gator poacher from Folkston, Barney ran the culprit down in his boat and subdued him with a chokehold, only to see him escape when his canoe sank. Barney said the poacher reached solid ground, pulled out his gun, and started shooting. Barney returned fire, but no one was wounded in the encounter.

Barney's life was once threatened by the species he fought so hard to protect. While cruising cat face timber on Cowhouse Island, he accidentally stepped on a large gator in the middle of a flooded firebreak. The gator grabbed Barney by the seat of the pants and began to roll him. He was able to grab a small cypress sapling and pull himself from the gator's viselike jaws.

Barney also told the story about how Chase Prairie got its name. He said that deer hunters using dogs would drive the animals onto the prairie, where hunters in pole boats would be waiting to chase down the escaping deer and dispatch them. I was surprised to learn that both deer and bear were not plentiful in the refuge in the early days of the USFWS occupation.

One of Barney's funniest stories involved revenue officers trying to apprehend a moonshiner. The still operator allegedly had a withered leg that caused him to bob up and down when he ran. As he ran from the officers, his head would rise above and then drop below the high grass. One of the revenue men, who didn't know the man's affliction, said, "Well, no sense in chasing him, he's got a horse."

The Okefenokee Swamp harbors many stories. A few people make them, many others just pass them on. Barney Cone has been in both camps. He will be sorely missed.

THE STORY OF ROUNDABOUT SWAMP

I have always been intrigued by swamps. I guess, because they reveal more faces than all the high cards in a deck of playing cards. Many swamps are dark, wet, mysterious places with a storied past. Rare birds, wildlife, plants, and trees find swamps very hospitable. Most of all, swamps are the most wild, natural places on earth.

No river feeds Roundabout Swamp—created by ancient geologic forces, altered by wild fires and loggers, and named by early overland traders—yet it has large wetland areas. When there is outflow, Little Red Bluff Creek is the recipient. Though Roundabout has discrete borders formed by roads, it is topographically connected to a continuous series of bays, swamps, and millponds in two counties.

I got an insider's tour of Roundabout from the Giddens family, who along with other family members own acreage in Roundabout.

The two large bays in Roundabout are Carolina bays, elliptical depressions in the earth, circular in shape, and having a northerly orientation. They were created thousands of years ago by the earth's forces. These shallow depressions have become isolated wetlands, largely fed by rain and ground water, and are hosts to trees like gum, cypress, bay, and maple and pond pine.

Though there was limited cutting on the edges of Roundabout in the early 1900s, it wasn't until the 1980s that a timber company built high canal roads through the bays to reach choice stands of virgin timber.

Ken Cook

Wildfires strike Roundabout about every fifteen to twenty years, and the last one in April 2007 destroyed 85% of the swamp's acreage, 2,000 acres of which burned on the first day. Mr. Giddens replanted his high-ground land with longleaf pine, swamp chestnut, and sawtooth oak, two fast-growing mast trees preferred by deer, turkey, and other wildlife.

A decade before the railroads crisscrossed South Georgia after 1830, steamboats and log rafts transported cotton, logs, and naval stores [turpentine] to the Georgia coast via navigable rivers such as the Ocmulgee and Altamaha. In both the eighteenth and nineteenth century, the job of transporting goods to and from small settlements located next to gristmills, turpentine stills, sawmills, and cotton gins fell on the shoulders of overland traders in horse- and oxen-drawn carts and wagons.

The shortest and most direct route to the inland settlements and the Gulf Coast led the first wagon traders smack into Roundabout swamp. This transportation barrier led to an old saying, "To get where you're going, you have to go 'round it or about it.

Wildfires and logging have left cosmetic scars in the bays, but birds and wildlife seem to be thriving. From the canal roads, we saw approximately seventy-five endangered wood storks, observed gray and white herons feeding, and jumped endless pairs of nesting waterfowl. Although we went around it and through it, Roundabout Swamp did not disappoint this outdoorsman.

Conservation

THE MOODY TRACT: ONE OF GEORGIA'S LAST FRONTIER FORESTS

The fate of Moody Forest came down to the slide of a letter opener. Bids for the purchase of this undisturbed 4,300 acre tract were being opened, and the Nature Conservancy's envelope lay at the bottom of the stack. When it was announced that the Nature Conservancy had won the bidding, collective applause could be heard all the way to Alligator Slough near the Altamaha River.

For those unfamiliar with Jake Moody and his three nephews or with the writings and actions of Janisse Ray, a Baxley, Georgia, native who championed the effort to save Moody Forest, you might wonder what the fuss was all about.

Home to the endangered red-cockaded woodpecker, gopher tortoise, and Indigo snake, Moody Forest is one of the three most ecologically important old-growth longleaf pine forests in Georgia. The preserve also contains the only known longleaf pine-blackjack oak stand in the country. Cypress up to six hundred years old and longleaf, slash, and loblolly pine two to three hundred years old populate Moody Forest.

It is hard to believe, but it is true that many cypress and tupelo gum trees in Moody Forest's river bottomland were growing when De Soto marched through in 1540. Creek and Cherokee tribes probably claimed this forest as part of their homeland, and Georgia settlers in the early 1700s no doubt marveled at these stately trees.

The Moody family began acquiring land in the mid-1800s. When Jake died in 1952, he willed the holdings to his nephews, Wade and Causs, and his niece, Elizabeth, along with their promise to live on the property and never cut the trees except to pay taxes.

As Jake had done before them, the nephews lived in primitive fashion, forsaking electricity, running water, and an indoor toilet. One fireplace provided the heat for the entire house. In Jake's lifetime, meager income was derived from turpentine and a small herd of cattle.

After Miss Elizabeth died in 1999, the Moody Tract fell to thirty heirs, and sale of the property became eminent. When the Nature Conservancy prevailed in the bidding and took ownership, they sold 1,700 acres to the Georgia Department of Natural Resources. Thus was created the first public-private land management partnership in the state of Georgia. Their shared mission is the restoration of the longleaf pine and conservation.

The first line of Joyce Kilmer's famous poem titled "Trees" sums up my visit to Moody Forest: "I think that I shall never see a poem as lovely as a tree." Kilmer's inspiration could easily have been Moody Forest.

TIS' THE SEASON FOR AN ECOTOUR

I t's hard being an outdoorsman in the summer time. So many things you'd like to do, but they're not in season or are too hot, too expensive, or too much trouble. So my wife and I set out in search of an outdoor adventure that was both enjoyable and different.

Ecotourism is a fast-growing segment of the tourism industry and usually involves travel to places where flora, fauna, and cultural heritage are the primary attractions. Las Vegas, fancy island resorts, and mammoth amusement parks didn't make our list, but Southwest Louisiana fit like Cinderella's slipper.

Acadiana is the name given to this five-parish region west of Baton Rouge. French immigrants from eastern Canada settled the area in the mid to late 1700s, and the Acadians, as they were originally called, became known as Cajuns. Here are a few of the highlights from our three-day Cajun Country ecotour.

MULATE'S IN BREAUX BRIDGE

We got a full baptism in Cajun culture on a Sunday night at this windowless restaurant and dance hall. Cajuns have their own brand of food, dancing, and music, and Mulate's served up ample quantities of all three. The songs, with French lyrics and a driving beat, drowned out all conversation; the dance floor never emptied; and multiple generations of families took turns doing the Cajun two-step.

ATCHAFALAYA BASIN

Now leveed by the Corps of Engineers to one million acres, the Atchafalaya Basin was once an ancient bay of the Gulf of Mexico and is now the largest river swamp in North America. If left undisturbed by the hand of man, the Mississippi River would empty into the Gulf through the Atchafalaya instead of New Orleans.

INDIAN BAYOU

Within the Basin is a Corps-operated, 28,000 acre, public access, natural area that is home to over two hundred species of birds, many threatened or endangered. The American Bird Conservancy has classified the area a Globally Important Bird Area. The verdant bottomland hardwood forests reflect a stunning diversity of wildlife habitats. Indian Bayou is also managed for hunting and fishing.

LAKE MARTIN AND CYPRESS ISLAND PRESERVE

Also close in to Breaux Bridge is Lake Martin, a naturally occurring open body of water within a cypress-tupelo swamp. On the western side of the lake is the Cypress Island Preserve, a 9,500 acre protected area owned by the Nature Conservancy. The preserve supports one of the largest colonial water-bird rookeries in North America.

Ken Cook

SHADOWS ON THE TECHE

In the town of New Iberia, adjacent to Teche Bayou, sits the historic plantation home and gardens of David Weeks, a sugar-cane planter, that date back to 1831–1834 and housed four generations of his family. Now operated by the National Trust, the house is a combination of classical revival style (exterior) and Louisiana colonial interior. The home contains an impressive collection of period furniture and is one of the best-documented tour experiences in the country.

JUNGLE GARDENS ON AVERY ISLAND

Though the Tabasco factory tour is a bit commercial, the McIlhenny family's two-hundred-acre Jungle Gardens is well worth the drive to Avery Island. E. A. McIlhenny, son of the Tabasco pepper sauce inventor, was a noted naturalist and explorer who helped save the snowy egret from extinction and created a nesting colony of 20,000 water birds, including blue herons and black ibises. A tall viewing platform allows visitors to leisurely watch these birds, and the complete story of the gardens will enthrall you.

What makes a well-chosen ecotour so sweet is that the whole family can participate, and members with outdoor interests can walk in (or drive through) and see natural areas that books and videos fail to convey. There are many affordable ecotour options for the outdoor family to pass the summertime, and plenty of time left to take one with your family.

BANKS LAKE NATIONAL WILDLIFE REFUGE: A NATURAL RESOURCE WORTHY OF NURTURING

They show up on a Georgia Atlas as elliptical-shaped bodies of water encased in lowland, wooded marsh. "They," in this instance, are alternately referred to as pocosins, sinks, millponds, and Carolina bays. Their creation was geological in origin and dates back thousands of years.

Proximity to Lanier County and the town of Lakeland is only one of the reasons Banks Lake National Wildlife Refuge has earned a position of prominence among these unique bodies of water. Dating back to the mid-1800s, Banks Lake and its environs have been a center of early commerce and trade, location for a popular movie, and an abundant provider of fish and wildlife.

I first fished Banks Lake in the mid-1970s and was taken by its beauty, wildlife, and historical heritage. After passage of almost four decades, I yearned for a reunion with Banks Lake.

The Chamber of Commerce was quick to oblige, and they arranged a boat tour with two longtime residents. Of no small assist in my discovery was Nell Roquemore's book, *Lanier County: The Land and Its People*, a brilliantly researched and skillfully presented history of the county.

Banks Lake is different from what I remember. In some ways positive and in other ways troubling. Some of the old "boat runs" connecting Banks Lake to Grand Bay

Ken Cook

and other areas of the larger ecosystem are now choked with bonnets, buttonwood bushes, and "mud mounds," masses which have broken loose from the lake bottom and now serve as floating seed beds for unwanted volunteer cypress trees and vegetation.

Mother Nature is clearly on a relentless quest to reclaim portions of Banks Lake's remaining open water. In a natural cycle, aquatic vegetation, if left unchecked, will eventually win this battle.

Although fishing for bass, bluegill, and other species is still good in "season," waterfowl hunting has declined significantly, and the rapid growth of the alligator population is a questionable enhancement to wildlife viewing and ecotourism

My time with the two guides and historians who both treasure Banks Lake left me with their concerns about the spread of aquatic vegetation and lake drawdowns deployed by the US Fish and Wildlife Service to help control aquatic plants.

Owned now by the US Fish and Wildlife Service and designated a National Wildlife Refuge, Banks Lake has no local funding nor is staffed as a stand-alone refuge. Staff and volunteers do all work from Okefenokee NWR, 125 miles away.

The Georgia Department of National Resources, Wildlife Resources Division, is responsible for monitoring fish populations, enforcing game and fish laws, and providing facilities for access.

I called the Okefenokee National Wildlife Refuge to see if Banks Lake is the focus of a management plan and learned from the public information officer that a comprehensive management plan (available to the public) is in place, and drawdowns are their primary tool for controlling vegetation. A drawdown is a manual lowering of the lake level to help eradicate aquatic plants. Drawdowns were implemented in 1984, 1994, 2001, 2007, and in the fall of 2011. A complete environmental assessment was conducted in 2007.

It was mentioned that prior to the fall 2011 drawdown, an open, public meeting was held in Lakeland, and numerous notifications were sent to public officials and the newspaper. Banks Lake refilled at the end of March 2012, two months before it was implemented.

Regardless of local sentiment on the threat from aquatic vegetation and drawdowns, Banks Lake NWR is a jewel. It's a beautiful outdoor playground responsible for 83,000 visitors each year and an economic driver for both the city and county.

But Banks Lake could use some tender loving care, and this might come through creation of a Friends of Banks Lake coalition in which citizens get involved, support, volunteer, and work in close partnership with USFWS.

As one well-known conservationist I know once said, "You don't get the resource you desire; you get the resource you fight for."

Ken Cook

Game

WARDENS

RIDING FOR THE BRAND

In a popular western movie, a well-known actor plays the role of a ranch hand who refuses to collaborate with his fellow cowhands in rustling his employer's herd. In a nose to nose showdown, the actor tells the disloyal cowhand that he won't be joining him in this nefarious act: "I'm riding for the brand." I've always remembered this line because it epitomized loyalty and commitment to the person for whom one works and for those whom they serve.

I recently rode with a man who has ridden for his brand for twelve years, and he rides for the Georgia Department of Natural Resources, Wildlife Resources Division, Law Enforcement Section brand. The ranger is a game warden assigned to enforce game laws in several South Georgia counties.

Dressed in a crisply pressed uniform, the ranger and I mounted up in his specially equipped, shiny black Ford F-150 with blue lights on top, and he picked me up at my guest quarters, the Helmstead Bed and Breakfast. It was the start of an average day for the ranger, but not for me.

Our first stop was a nearby unoccupied hunt camp where a fellow ranger, a K-9 officer based in an adjacent county, demonstrated his dog's skill at recovering a spent shell casing and a discarded shotgun. K-9 dogs are often called on to recover evidence, find hidden game and lost people, and protect their handlers. K-9 dogs wear badges and are officially considered state law enforcement officers.

The ranger's K-9 dog, Gauge, took all of ten minutes to sniff out and locate both the hidden spent shell and

Ken Cook

the shotgun, using only his nose and the faintest scent of gunpowder.

With the second day of Georgia's bear season in full swing, we motored south to check bear hunters. Wildfires in the Okefenokee Refuge had black bears on the move, and hunters and their dogs were in hot pursuit. At the check-in station, the attendant was working double-time, and two state-record bears (598 and 600 pounds) had been weighed-in at separate locations in the county.

Enforcing Georgia's game laws is a dangerous occupation. In recent years, the force has lost a ranger about every four years, yet wardens pursue their job with absolute dedication. Always being on call, working long hours for a salary not commensurate with the job, and threatening confrontations just seem to go with the territory.

In the early days, game wardens had few tools to work with—a vehicle, a badge, a gun, and a two-way radio—a thin margin of safety for the officer. Rangers are now being equipped with an onboard computer system that allows them to perform all the tasks that state troopers do.

During my ride with the game warden, I witnessed the observation powers of a hawk, the intuition of Sherlock Holmes, the diplomacy of an ambassador, and the judgment of a wise ruler. Enforcement is situational and interpretative, I believe. "Educating and working with the public to gain voluntary compliance is often the better course of action to follow," the game warden told me. His comment confirmed that he still rides for the brand.

SAPELO TURTLE EGG THIEF
NABBED BY DNR

S core one big "collar" for the law enforcement officers of Region 7 who patrol Georgia's coastal waters between South Carolina and the Florida border. Superb and dogged investigative work resulted in the arrest of an alleged turtle-nest robber smuggling 156 endangered loggerhead turtle eggs from Sapelo Island.

Loggerhead turtles are the predominant species of sea turtle that nests on the beaches of Georgia's barrier islands each year between May and September. These and other species of sea turtles are listed as "threatened" under the Endangered Species Act of 1973.

According to the senior wildlife biologist with the conservation section, there are currently over 1,069 active sea turtle nests on Georgia beaches, of which thirty nests are on Sapelo. "We became suspicious when we found that four nests on Sapelo had been disturbed," the biologist said.

The usual threats to nests come from coyotes, feral hogs, and raccoons, not humans. "It is a fairly rare occurrence when humans disturb nests and poach eggs, but it has happened," the senior biologist added. The maximum penalty for disturbing nests can be a $10,000 fine and jail time.

Beyond the natural threats to sea turtle nests, there is a 40% mortality rate among hatchlings in an average-sized clutch of 115 eggs. Among those that emerge from the sand, there is an undocumented number that don't survive the dash to the ocean.

Ken Cook

Acting on fresh intelligence, Region 7 law enforcement officers set up a wildlife checkpoint at the Meridian, Georgia, ferry, which provides service to Sapelo. Among the officers on hand at the dock was Gauge, a K-9 dog brought in to "sniff" for wildlife contraband.

As passengers disembarked with their luggage, each was questioned while Gauge worked the luggage. In short order, Gauge "alerted" his ranger handler that contraband was probably present. Inside a duffle bag belonging to a passenger, 156 loggerhead turtle eggs were found, neatly sorted in zip-closure bags.

Gauge is a remarkable K-9, and I had the privilege of watching him work when I wrote a column last year after a ranger ride-along. I watched in awe as Gauge miraculously located a spent shot shell and a discarded shotgun. DNR K-9s are trained to locate guns and wildlife evidence, but not drugs.

A duffle bag full of kudos should be presented to the Georgia Department of Natural Resources law enforcement officers of Region 7. Captain Lewis, who heads up the Region 7 Law Enforcement Section of the Wildlife Resources Division, modestly gives the credit to his team of officers.

A postscript to this caper is that the smuggled loggerhead eggs were reportedly destined for sale to area residents, for twenty to forty dollars per egg, to be consumed raw for their perceived benefit as an aphrodisiac.

Outdoor
CRAFTSMEN

ART FROM STEEL AND BONE

Known among his peers as the "hardest working knife maker in the business," Mr. Pridgen, age forty-five, always seems to be operating in overdrive. Often rising at 3:30 a.m. to get in two hours of work before he leaves for his day job, Pridgen proudly says, "I work forty hours a week in a sawmill and still manage to build twenty knives a month."

Several years back, using nothing more than a hand-held drill and a Craftsman sander, Pridgen fashioned a straight-bladed, steel skinning knife from an ordinary file and attached a handle made of deer antler. Though he considered it crude, his craftsmanship was visible to knife enthusiasts, and his company was born.

Today, in a cluttered workshop behind his home, Pridgen designs and produces a variety of custom implements, including large Bowie knives, folding knives, skinning knives, tomahawks, cane knives, push knives, and a few swords. Half of his output is folders and skinners. On his table at a typical out of town knife show will be knives priced between $200 and $1,250, though some items may occasionally range as high as $5,000.

Pridgen's custom knives have grown in popularity and demand among collectors and users over the years. "I have one customer who owns 350 of my knives, and another collector in Europe has a standing order for almost every knife design that I put up," Pridgen explains. After three years of designing and building knives, he was elected to membership in the prestigious American Knife Makers

Guild, and two of his custom designs were included in the thirty-first annual edition of the *World's Greatest Knife Book*.

Dark in color, Damascus steel is the primary component that gives his knives their genuinely unique, one-of-a-kind beauty. Hammer-forged, multilayered Damascus steel is preferred for its hardness and ease of sharpening, but is also expensive and difficult to source. A chemical "etching" process leaves extraordinary designs/imprints on the surface of the metal, many of which have been given descriptive names like dragon skin, raindrops, and twisted chain.

The finishing touch on a custom knife is the material used for the handle or accents. These materials range from wooly mammoth tusks (dug from glaciers), wild hog tusk, ram horn, armadillo, and a host of other woods and bone. Pridgen's wife sews pouches for each folding knife, and leather scabbards are outsourced.

I asked him if custom knives appreciate over time. "When I first started, I was selling my knives for $30 to $50, and I'm now paying $200 to $250, on average, to buy back those same knives for my portfolio." Not all of his knives are collector grade; he also makes hunting knives and skinners. Knife art assumes many forms.

IS IT REAL OR MOUNTED?

The first buck I ever killed was mounted in 1972 by a wildlife biologist and part-time taxidermist. He did a satisfactory job on it, and the shoulder mount has held up pretty well over the past forty-two years. I recently talked to two taxidermists to see what changes have taken place in their business over the past four decades.

Cally Morris, of Hazel Creek Taxidermy in Missouri, is a world-champion taxidermist. I caught up with him at the National Wild Turkey Convention in Nashville, Tennessee. In the course of five years, he walked away with the top prize in North American, Grand National, and World Taxidermy Competitions.

Morris told me the most significant advances in taxidermy occurred in the last twenty years, and he outlined three major trends: 1) Better materials to work with. Mannequins or forms, to which hides and feathers are attached, reflect astounding anatomical detail. Eyes, nose, ear liners, and other artificial parts are exceptionally realistic these days. 2) Better tanning of hides and adhesives to fit skins to forms. Taxidermists have also sharpened their skills at preparing skins and feathers. "With fur animals, mount them and make them pretty; with feathers, make them pretty before mounting" according to Cally. 3) Greater artistic expression in taxidermy. Presentation of wildlife mounts in their natural habitats is very much in vogue today. This is also the reason many mounts have earned a place in the den or trophy room, rather than a dusty corner of the garage. Customers are demanding more artistic interpretation from their taxidermists. Cabinetry, rocks, soil, trees, and all manner of flora are now standard components of wildlife mounts.

Matt Pittman, a full-time taxidermist who owns Pittman's Taxidermy Studio confirmed these trends. The mounts in his display room reflect his sharp eye for detail and his talent for artistic expression. Most of his work features deer and fish, but it extends to bear, hog, waterfowl, and small mammals. Matt holds both state and federal taxidermy licenses.

Matt said, "The first two questions people always ask are: How soon can I get it [the mount] and how much will it cost?" For customers whose hunting trips often exceed a thousand dollars, it's penny wise and pound foolish to cut corners on a mount that memorializes a hunt of a life time.

Though it isn't the most enjoyable part of taxidermy, Matt says that doing his own skinning yields better results in the final product. He seeks perfection in his mounts, and this requires daily tweaking before he finally steps back and says, "It is ready."

Talk with your taxidermist and check out their display mounts *before* your next hunting or fishing trip. It'll be time wisely spent.

Ken Cook

THE SOUND OF AN ARTIST

I was not prepared when I turned into the driveway leading to Jerry White's neat country home and workshop in eastern Georgia. We had previously met at a Labor Day dove shoot, and I was following the address on his business card that reads Dad's Custom Box Calls. That's about all I knew.

Very quickly, I realized I had just raised the lid on Pandora's Box. For inside was a true craftsman plying his trade creating and building wild turkey callers, an endeavor described by Howard Harlan as "enduring American folk art."

My eyes began to widen as Jerry toured me through a maze of connected small buildings housing exotic woods, rows of woodworking machines, stacks of boxed products ready for shipping, a final assembly table manned by his trusted assistant, and Jerry's personal call collection worthy of museum status. I'm not sure what I expected, but I was blown away by what I observed and heard.

Jerry White, a soft-spoken, modest man dressed in camouflage bib overalls and ball cap, wasn't always a turkey-call maker. He was in the construction business for forty years, and his large, weathered hands provide proof. The demands of the construction business and his addiction to turkey hunting, which began in 1985, set Jerry on a new career path—creating and perfecting custom turkey calls. He built his first friction box call in 1997.

Although call makers are traditionally close-mouthed about their call-building process for fear of knock-offs, I observed factors that enable Jerry to excel at his business. The construction business taught him problem-solving and the know-how to adapt common woodworking machines to the intricate steps (fifty-four in all) involved in turning blocks of wood into items of beauty, consistency, and performance.

"Anybody can make a box call, but to make it sound like a turkey on both sides is what makes it special; I won't sell a call that doesn't sound like a turkey," Jerry said with conviction.

Holder of five Grand Slams in turkey hunting and one of the first call makers to have a web site (www.dadscalls.com), Jerry next expanded into the pot and striker call category quite by accident. He was turkey hunting in Montana with a call maker who ran short of money and traded his inventory of pots and strikers to cover the shortage.

Dad's Custom Calls has never stopped innovating, expanding, and experimenting since its beginning. Drawing from twenty-eight different species of wood and four different species in his lid paddles, the ability to marry different woods to produce different tones is truly the work of an artisan. The perfect marriage, according to Jerry, is a box made of cedar with a Purple Heart wood paddle.

Though Jerry's product line is anchored in box calls, it also includes air-operated trumpet calls, long boxes, and a limited edition, hand-painted, and personalized collector's series of box calls. Hand-sewn holsters are made by his assistant, and her husband turns the strikers, also made from exotic woods.

Ken Cook

Part III:

FISHING

Freshwater
FISHING

DYLAN AND THE GIANT GARFISH

Dylan is an adorable, engaging youngster who lives in Ohio. Although he loves outdoor activities, his parents don't have much time to take him fishing because they are busy working and raising Dylan's sibling twins. Dylan's grandfather, Gary Fleming, a Wichita resident, is a consummate sportsman who gladly stepped in and became Dylan's outdoor mentor.

Late last summer, Grandpa Fleming and a friend from Rose Hill, Kansas, hatched a plan to take Dylan on a Midwestern "big game" fishing trip. The friend, by the way, is a noted gar fisherman with bow and arrow. He and Gary thought it would be fun for Dylan to face off with a prehistoric holdover known as a longnose gar. The world record longnose weighed in at fifty pounds and measured upwards of seventy inches.

Gary's friend knew a perfect place to find garfish. The trio loaded up and drove to the stained tail waters of a dam on the nearby Walnut River.

Filled with anticipation and curiosity, Dylan asked to see a gar lure and wanted a description on how it was made. Here is the answer his grandpa gave: Cut four strands of stranded nylon trotline about fourteen inches in length and thread them through the lower eye of a double-eye barrel swivel. Secure by crimping the strands just below the eye with copper flashing material. This adds weight and color. Then fray out the strands. No hooks are needed and the lure will weigh about three-eighths of an ounce.

Outfitted with a six-foot five-inch, flex-tip rod and spinning reel spooled with 12# monofilament line, Dylan was instructed to walk the bank, cast, and slowly reel the homemade gar lure back to him. When the gar strikes, give him slack and the fish will hook itself and begin rolling like an alligator, his rows of tiny teeth becoming hopelessly entangled in the stranded and frayed nylon cord.

Ten casts later, a twenty-minute tussle erupted between Dylan and a monster garfish that any adult angler would have stood in line for. With bent rod and thrashing fish, Dylan held steady pressure on the fish and skillfully guided the defeated gar to the bank. Gary's friend, whom Dylan call "Mr. John," was there with gloved hands to lift the giant from the water as Dylan caught his breath and tried to speak. It was high-five time.

Fellow classmates may never top Dylan's "show and tell" story, nor will he ever forget this experience. His giant garfish weighed eighteen pounds and stretched fifty-eight inches long, a full six inches taller than Dylan. Thanks to Dylan's mentors and fishing guides, this kid's hooked on fishing for life.

YOU GET A LINE AND I'LL GET A POLE

And we'll go down to the crawdad hole, read the lyrics of an old folk song. I was seven years old when I first held a mechanical fishing rod and reel. Pap owned a Pflueger bait-casting reel seated on a four-foot steel rod. Green braided line was wound on the reel, and a yellow Hawaiian Wiggler lure was tied on the business end of this fish-catching contraption. Pap liked to walk the banks of Jones Creek and cast under the overhanging branches for "green trout."

Even though Pap owned a rod and reel, he used it infrequently. Our family members were born and bred, true blue, bamboo cane pole fishermen. We rarely fished from a boat because Mama couldn't swim. Our comfort zone was the banks of small streams, rivers, and farm ponds near our Southern Mississippi home.

Mama dearly loved to fish; in fact, fishing was her chief interest outside home and family. Though she feared fishing from a jon boat, she treasured the trips to Logtown, Mississippi, where bayou backwaters yielded pole-bending fish of various species.

There is still something mystical about a whippy, ten-foot cane pole rigged with care and precision. I used to watch hypnotically as my father tied monofilament line two feet from the tip, wrapped the knot with black electric tape, wound the line back to the pole's tip, tied a knot at the tip, and wrapped that knot with tape. His methodology ensured that the pole would bend rather than break when a "whopper" took the bait.

Pap then stripped line from the spool and carefully snipped it six inches below the butt end of the pole. Like a surgeon preparing to operate, he took from a small paper sack a short-shank bream hook, two tiny lead sinkers, and a small cork. When these items were attached in their proper locations, Pap wound the line down the pole and secured the point of the hook under adhesive tape at the end of the pole. For cane pole fishing, a tackle box was the small brown paper sack used by the retailer to hold the items you had purchased. Pap kept his "tackle sack" rolled up and stowed in his left front shirt pocket.

Technological innovations designed to increase fishing success (and tackle sales) now drive the fishing tackle industry, and "new" is the operative word that sends us racing to fishing tackle outlets and catalogs to purchase the newest gear. Even the lowly bamboo cane pole has not escaped this trend. There are now telescoping fiberglass poles made for bream and crappie fishermen.

Technology aside, there is something therapeutic and nostalgic about rigging a bamboo cane pole the way your father taught you and then settling back in your lawn chair and watching the cork. You owe it to your kids and grandkids to take them fishing and introduce them to low-tech bank fishing with a cane pole.

If this approach doesn't hold their interest, however, there are suitable and acceptable alternatives. The famous Zebco 33 spin-casting reel, first introduced in 1952 and still going strong, is a surefire solution. And if your kids are very young and need additional coaxing, try a Zebco Dora the Explorer or SpongeBob fishing kit.

Ken Cook

THE REDBREAST BROTHERHOOD

Satilla River redbreast lie low when Bobby Brooker is on the river. He knows where they hang out; knows how to fool them into biting; and knows how to welcome them aboard his well-used but comfortable fourteen-foot aluminum jon boat. My jaw dropped when I saw him pull a "rooster red" from a patch of water no bigger than the crown of my Tilley hat. Bobby's good. Real good.

After four decades of fishing, Bobby is in a class of elite pan-fish anglers that I call the Redbreast Brotherhood. There is no membership roll, no charter, and no meetings in this conclave, yet they all know each other. What they have in common is a passion for redbreast fishing and a level of friendly, unspoken competition so subtle it often goes unnoticed.

When you step into a boat equipped with a chainsaw, you know you're in for close quarters fishing. I'm no stranger to fishing narrow, black water Georgia rivers, but Bobby's style of fishing for redbreast is "target casting," requiring precision, feel, and courage. "Don't get frustrated about getting hung up," Bobby reassured me. "If you don't get hung up, you're not fishing in the right places," he added.

Gear selection for redbreast in the Satilla is acquired over years of trial and error, and won't be found in a tackle store with a hangtag reading, "Redbreast Rig." Bobby fishes four to five feet custom one-piece rods equipped with Zebco Ultra Lite spin cast reels smaller than a man's fist. They are spooled with Stren Magna Thin six-pound line, which has the break-strength of an eight pound and the diameter of a four pound. On the business end of this rig is tied a 1/32 oz. jig head, a small, tailless plastic grub, and a brass spinner with a tiny Colorado blade. Color choice varies widely.

Over the course of our four-hour trip, we both landed a respectable number of redbreast, bream, and "stump knockers," including one grumpy mudfish. What impressed me most, however, was Bobby's concern for perpetuation of the redbreast species. He released every juvenile and egg-laying female with a "see you next year" send off. Bobby has a self-imposed rule of not keeping any redbreast under six inches in length and weighing less than a pound.

I asked him about the flathead catfish threat to redbreasts and posed the question in the form of a 1 to 10 rating over the past twenty years. Twenty years ago, the Altamaha and Satilla would have been a 10. Today the Altamaha is a .5 to 1.5, and the Satilla is an eight. Bobby is also not opposed to DNR size restrictions to help protect this valuable resource.

I'm under oath not to reveal the location we fished, but I will close with a Brooker-ism. "When the yellow flies land and gather on your outside truck mirrors on the way to the landing, cock your pistol son, cause the redbreasts are gonna be biting today," he said. Long live these beautiful game fish and fishermen like Bobby Brooker.

Saltwater
FISHING

Wild Country

PURA PESCADO EN COSTA RICA

Poorly translated from Spanish, the phrase means plenty of fish in Costa Rica. Due to a lucky draw and expenses franked, I joined a small group of anglers traveling to Crocodile Bay Fishing Resort near Port Jimenez on the Pacific side of this Central American country. I was no stranger to Costa Rican fishing. I went there in the mid-1980s to fish for tarpon on the Caribbean side of the country. This trip, however, we were chasing fish I had never landed before—roosterfish and marlin in particular.

Crocodile Bay is a beautiful fishing destination, endorsed by Orvis, Cabela's, and Gander Mountain. It's located at the end of the Osa Peninsula leading into the Pacific Ocean. Food, service, and lodging were first class, and if you time it right, fishing is excellent.

Getting there was fairly easy—a four-hour, nonstop flight from Atlanta to San Jose, the capital, followed by an overnight stay and a second flight (fifty minutes) the following morning over the mountains and rainforest to Port Jimenez. Language was never a barrier, and we were escorted at all times. We arrived late morning in time to check in, have lunch, and fish for a few hours.

I fished from a twenty-six-foot, diesel-powered Rambo boat with center console, one of the last three built by a Florida builder. Though it had some age, it was a smooth, dry ride and well designed for inshore bottom fishing and near-shore ocean trolling and plugging. Fishing tackle and electronics on board were all familiar brands—Hummingbird,

Ken Cook

Okuma, and Shimano spinning and bait-casting reels; Lamiglas rods; line and leaders by Trilene and Sufix; and Eagle Claw circle hooks.

Captain Anthony, a Bronx-born Hispanic, and the first mate, Jose, knew where to find fish. Choose your species, quality over quantity, and catch and release are the options extended to you by Crock Bay guides. Edible fish like snapper (red, yellow, and Cubera) and pompano are boated, filleted, and delivered to the kitchen for each night's dinner meal.

On the first afternoon, using live bait, I boated an African Pompano and hooked up with a crevalle while bottom fishing in seventy-five feet of water. Jacks can go a full fifteen rounds with an angler, and in the humid climate, with insufficient hydration and jet lag, I lasted ten rounds. I handed the rod to the mate and called it a day.

Our second day was spectacular, capped off with two roosterfish up to 38#, a 15# Colorado snapper, and another jack. The Captain piloted our boat into the middle of several humpback whales that were circling a school of bonita. A giant humpback surfacing fifty yards from our boat was heart-stopping. Catches on the last fishing day included a yellowfin tuna, which was filleted on board with snack portions passed around.

Although the rainy season nixed our offshore fishing for sail and marlin, our catch was varied and very sporting. If you plan a trip, go in December and January, the high season. The fishing is unique and the scenery is stunning.

JUST ABOUT AS GOOD AS IT GETS

T he e-mail from my nephew was short and sweet: "Better get on down to Shellman; the tides are right, winds are moderate, and we should catch some fish over the next three days." That's all the encouragement I needed to strike out on a six-hour drive to Shellman Bluff on the Georgia coast. After all, it was also our family's annual fall fishing trip.

The early morning run on day one from Fisherman's Lodge marina to Blackbeard Creek in our twenty-foot Ranger bay boat was chilly but loaded with anticipation. The new Buff headgear and gloves we wore made the run across Sapelo Sound surprisingly tolerable.

To be successful in inshore fishing at Shellman, you have to know the tides and fish the tidal changes. For spotted sea trout, we usually work the edges of spartina grass and small drainage openings terminating in the main creek channel. At low tide, exposed oyster bars will hold redfish.

Light tackle is always our preference, and the four adults in our boat were armed to the teeth with Quantum EXO and Shimano Stradic spinning reels spooled with Berkley Nanofil braid and fluorocarbon lines and leaders. Fast action, whippy EXO and St. Croix rods were our bait-delivery systems.

To bracket the fish-biting options, we chose Berkley Gulp Saltwater soft bait jigs, DOA plastic shrimp, and live shrimp. Baits were tied to four-foot leaders and jerk floats. It didn't seem to matter what bait we used because every angler was bringing spotted sea trout to the boat.

We quit fishing around midafternoon and our scorecard was thirty-two trout up to seventeen inches and two keeper redfish. We must have caught and released three times as many trout under the thirteen-inch limit.

Day two brought the arrival of a second boat—a twenty-two-foot Navistar bay boat piloted by another nephew and two young, sub-teen boys. The angler count was now five adults and two youngsters. Refusing to tamper with success, we fished the same areas using the same gear and baits. We fished longer and harder on day two and ended up boating a total of fifty-three trout. A family friend prepared a celebratory dinner of squash fries, steamed local shrimp, coleslaw, and fried trout fillets with hush puppies. BAM!

Day three ushered in some experimentation with bait-casting reels and different choices of jigged soft baits. The Berkley Gulp Saltwater soft plastics continued to be highly productive, especially the Nuclear Chicken color pattern.

The day three creel count was forty-three trout up to twenty inches in length. Over the three-day trip, we took home 128 fish—123 trout and five reds. We estimated that we had released two to three times that many fish that were undersized.

Our fishing trip was just about as good as it gets, and fishing with three generations of family members is definitely a keeper.

FISHFUL THINKING

The name on the side of the boat "Fishful Thinking Guide Service" should have tipped me off as to how this half-day inshore charter was going to end. But I was too busy thinking about the forty-pound bull red the captain said they brought on board the day before. After all, there are no bad fishing days.

I was in South Carolina attending the annual conclave of the South Carolina Outdoor Writers Association. Two colleagues and I were booked for a half-day of inshore fishing out of Murrells Inlet, a fabled fishing village just south of Myrtle Beach on the Atlantic Ocean.

Captain Baish pushed his twenty-four-foot Key West away from the public dock and slowly motored to a nearby area where he cast for baitfish. With enough in the bait well, he throttled his twin 150-HP Yamaha engines seven miles down the beach and anchored the boat in the same spot where the forty-pound redfish was caught the day before. We were barely a stone's throw from the sandy beach framed by high-rise condos and seven feet of water.

Using PENN Battle 4000 spinning reels and Ugly Stick rods, we cast cut bait from both sides of the boat and bumped the rigs along the bottom. The terminal rig consisted of a one-ounce egg sinker above a barrel swivel that was tied to a ten-inch mono leader. The reel spool was wound with braided line.

Two hours of fishing produced two four-foot Atlantic sharp-nosed sharks and three weakfish (gray or summer trout). Time to move. Our next stop was three miles out

Ken Cook

over a manmade reef that should have been holding hungry flounder, snapper, and grouper.

Using the same rigs and fishing in thirty-five-feet of water with small, live mullet didn't produce better results than our previous spot. It was time to reel in and head for the dock. Captain Baish apologized profusely, but unnecessarily. Theoretically, we had all been there before.

Exactly thirteen days later, I found myself in Sarasota, Florida at a writer's conference sponsored by the Theodore Roosevelt Conservation Partnership. And yes, a half-day, light-tackle fishing trip in the bay and Gulf was on the agenda. Could it be that this was the road to redemption for striking out in South Carolina?

Captain Burkhart was piloting a twenty-two-foot Triton boat powered by a 200-HP Mercury engine. Shimano spinning reels and rods was his choice for weaponry, and DOA soft plastic baits, with jig heads, were tied on small diameter monofilament with a fluorocarbon leader. His technique was sight fishing for schooling baitfish and hurling the jigs into the schools. Water depth in the bay was nine feet.

Burkhart's technique was productive but painstakingly slow. We did manage to catch some Spanish mackerel, sea trout, ladyfish, and one jack, but we had to compete with pesky cormorant birds and dolphins. Our trip was enjoyable but could hardly be described as full redemption. Such is fishing.

Bass
FISHING

THE HUNT FOR TIGER BASS

I felt my ears twitch and rotate forward like a chased rabbit when Mr. Williamson, the owner, casually mentioned that his lakes were stocked with "Tiger Bass." Driven to backfill this void in my piscatorial repertory, I rudely leaned into his space and asked for a definition.

In fewer words than this, he explained that tiger bass had been specially bred for aggressiveness and fast growth and were capable of gaining more than two pounds per year. American Sport Fish of Montgomery, Alabama, a firm that breeds, stocks, and manages the six ponds on his property added that this fish was a cross between two pure subspecies of bass—Northern bass and Florida largemouth bass.

An outdoor writer/photographer and I quickly volunteered when offered a chance to fish for tiger bass. He and I were part of an eight-person contingent of outdoor writers and photographers invited to sample the sporting options available at a large plantation in the Red Hills region of North Central Florida.

Accompanied by one of the plantation's experienced guides, we bank-fished from wide, well-groomed shorelines (ideal for both fly and conventional angling) surrounding all of the property's scenic ponds. In one of the lakes, we began to hook up with hungry bass, and within an hour and a half, we caught and released five healthy largemouth bass weighing up to five pounds.

The following afternoon, another guide drove us to the honey hole and principal lair of tiger bass. Sleep did not come easy for either my writer friend or I the night before.

Practically every second or third cast into the lake produced a firm, positive response at the end of the line. We quickly learned that a hook set should immediately follow line tension because, when tiger Bass bite, they don't dilly dally around—they inhale it.

The choice of lures didn't seem to matter much to these bass, although a Zoom June Bug soft worm, Texas-rigged, rang the dinner bell loudest. A slow, bouncing retrieve worked best in attracting these predators because the water temperature was cool.

Part way through our trip, fishing ceased when our guide spotted a lone bobwhite quail perched on a rafter beneath a shelter that extended out into the lake. Momentarily, my thoughts shifted to the excellent quail hunt we had experienced two mornings prior.

Quentin the Quail, as we named the bird, dropped down on the dock from his perch, only a few feet away from me, and casually began to feed on loose fish food pellets under a feeder at the end of the dock. I interpreted Quentin's actions as a metaphor for the abundance of wild game and fish that harmoniously exist at this beautiful plantation.

Ken Cook

A WORLD RECORD STILL STANDING
AFTER EIGHTY YEARS

On a desolate stretch of blacktop road seven miles from the one-traffic-light town of Jacksonville, Georgia, stands a historical marker of great significance in the freshwater sport fishing world. The marker attests to the World's Largest Bass caught by George Perry in June of 1932. It's a record that has stood for eighty years.

Finding Montgomery Lake, a backwater body of water off the main run of the Ocmulgee River, proved as elusive as Perry's trophy largemouth. Although it is located somewhere on the Horse Creek Wildlife Management Area, no visible signs or forest roads are marked with the name Montgomery Lake.

Sport fishing was not the primary reason that directed Perry and his fishing buddy, J. E. Page, to Montgomery Lake on June 2, 1932—it was to catch a mess of fish to feed Perry's family of six. The Great Depression was raging, and fishing and hunting put food on the dinner table.

Equipped with only one rod, reel, and lure—a Creek Chub Fintail Shiner—the two pushed their homemade boat away from the bank and into the water. They took turns casting and sculling the boat.

According to the account Perry gave a sports writer with *Sports Afield* magazine in 1969, Perry saw a disturbance near a stump and made a cast to it. "All at once water splashed everywhere and I reared back and tried to reel but nothing happened, then the fish moved and the fight was on; what had me worried was losing the lure," Perry said.

Recognizing that neither angler had ever seen a bass this large, they took the fish to a general store in nearby Helena, Georgia, where it measured thirty-two-and-a-half inches long and twenty-eight-and-a-half inches around. Next, the fish was taken to the local post office where it topped the certified scales at twenty-two pounds and four ounces.

Having heard of a big fish contest sponsored by *Field & Stream*, which Perry entered and won handily, his catch has stood the test of time even when no organizations were keeping official records. The International Game Fish Association (IGFA) shows Perry's largemouth as being an All-Tackle World Record in the category.

In 2009, the bass fishing world was stunned when Manabu Kurita tied Perry's record with a twenty-two pound, four ounce largemouth taken from Lake Biwa near Shiga, Japan.

Although angler-envy, passage of time, and the lack of photographic evidence have generated a lot of controversy about the authenticity of Perry's world record bass, he still sits atop the record books and the State of Georgia thought it was good enough to make the largemouth bass its state fish.

MY LATE SUMMER BASSIN' TRIP

I t's downright embarrassing to work in the sport fishing industry and rarely go fishing. When people learn what I do for a living, they always say, "Wow. What a great job you have; you must go on a lot of fishing trips." Regrettably, I seem to spend more time writing about fishing than actually going fishing.

Late summer, when the temperatures in South Georgia hang around ninety plus degrees, it is not the most opportune time to go bass fishing. Spawning phases are over, and bass are leaner. The water in shallow-water ponds is warm. The oxygen content is lower, which usually drives the bass into cooler, deeper water and slows their feeding activity until late in the day or early in the morning. I knew all this, but then I had the weekend off, and by golly, nothing could stop me from going. Rain, shine, cold, or hot—go whenever you can is my motto. And besides, I had a bunch of new lures to try out. No excuses.

I'm fortunate in having access to a private, six-acre farm pond built by "mule and drag" in the late 1940s. It is a healthy spring-fed pond from which several ten-pound bass have been taken in the last few years. I borrowed a jon boat equipped with trolling motor and fish finder and cast off as soon as I reached my destination that afternoon.

On my fourth cast, using a new Sebile Bull Crank shallow-running hard bait that I got in the mail two days earlier, I saw a large swirl in the water as a chunky bass engulfed the lure, and I set the hook. The line ripped through the water as the bass jumped three times and made desperate runs to dislodge the treble hook. All I could do was direct traffic and keep the bass from wrapping the line around the blades of the MotorGuide trolling motor.

When I finally boated the bass, I weighed him, removed the trebles, and gently released him back into the water. My Rapala digital scale recorded an even five pounds. As I often do, I whispered my short prayer of thanks for the gift, caught my breath, and raised my expectations.

Before darkness caught up with me and pushed me toward the launch, I had tried all three rod and reel combos (bait casting and two spinning) and can't-miss lures such as a blue crawfish soft bait, a six-inch watermelon plastic worm, a blue and chrome top water jerk bait, and a gaudy spinner bait that bore more colors than a rainbow.

At the end of my first afternoon, I had boated three more bass ranging in size from one and three quarters to three pounds—all in a span of two-and-a-half hours of fishing. I fished three more times over the weekend and hooked and released six more, one of which topped the scales at just over four pounds. The bite was slow in the mornings, but the afternoons made up for it.

Like I always say, whenever you can get away and go fishing (or hunting), GO! And don't forget to take a kid along.

Ken Cook

Part IV:

GAME BIRDS

Turkey
HUNTING

A VERY RARE WILD TURKEY

When he approached the wood line on his uncle's farm forty minutes before daybreak, Daniel, aged seventeen, didn't have the faintest clue what lay in store for him that Saturday morning in the spring of 2010.

Four gobbling toms soon interrupted the silence, and Daniel judged their distance to be 300 yards. He rapidly halved the distance, staked a decoy twenty-five yards away, and set up. Using his Primos Jackpot glass slate to announce his presence, Daniel let go with soft purrs and hen yelps, which set off a barrage of gobbles. And then the toms went silent.

A curious hen appeared on Daniel's left and craned her neck to locate the intruder. Daniel began "cutting" with his mouth call, but no gobbler responded until a cooperative woodpecker forced an approaching tom to "shock gobble." The longbeard was not only close but had also begun to "spit 'n drum" and rustle leaves by dragging the tips of his wing feathers.

With rays of sunlight penetrating the tree canopies and obscuring Daniel's vision, the gobbler's white head and beard finally came into view at forty-five yards. The bird was in full strut and took what seemed like hours to reach a comfortable shooting distance of twenty-five yards. Daniel flattened the tom with his Benelli M2 3" magnum and Winchester High-Density #4 duck loads left over from an Arkansas waterfowl trip.

All of Daniel's sensory systems momentarily shut down when he reached the fallen gobbler. He stared, shivered, and choked up in disbelief. Before him lay a wild turkey the likes of which he had never seen before. After Daniel steadied his hands, he called his uncle and then his father and stammered, "I just killed a white turkey. He's not normal; he's white." For the next year, the true identity of the white turkey remained a mystery.

Bobby Jones Taxidermy in Baxley was chosen to mount the Raulerson white turkey, and I was called and invited down to see the bird. Bobby cleared the interview and article with Mr. Raulerson, Daniel's father, and we all met at Bobby's shop. I was unprepared for the viewing of this strange-colored turkey, stunningly mounted in a gobbling position on a tree limb.

After the picture taking and interview, I immediately e-mailed a photo of the bird to Kevin Lowrey, Wildlife Biologist and Turkey Specialist with the DNR office in Gainesville. I also e-mailed Lovett Williams, a nationally known and published wildlife biologist and turkey expert (now deceased) in Florida.

Both biologists identified the turkey as a "smoke gray," one of four color mutations in wild turkeys. The other three color abnormalities are black (melanistic), reddish (erythritic), and white (albino). Raulerson's bird has white breast feathers and secondary wing feathers with black tips, solid black secondary tail feathers, and normal coloration on his primary wing feathers and tail, though the latter is white-tipped like a Merriam's species.

Lowrey, who said he has never seen a smoke gray, noted that 95% of smoke gray turkeys are hens, and a gobbler is a rarity. "How often color mutation occurs in wild turkey populations varies by subgroup but can be as frequent as 0.2%," Kevin added. The smoke gray shows up more often in South Carolina and Mississippi than in Georgia.

Williams, who had personally collected two smoke gray specimens in his career, described the bird as a partial albino mutant whose coloration is caused by a recessive gene. "If the bird mated with a normal-colored hen, offspring would be normal colored," he said. Williams estimated the incidence of a smoke gray gobbler in the general population to be one in 2,700 to 3,600 birds.

A WILD TURKEY FOR THE RECORD BOOK

I n a span of six short years, Mr. Durrance has become a remarkable turkey hunter. Remarkable in the sense that he killed a rare "black turkey" (melanistic) last spring and remarkable in his approach to hunting these Kings of the Forest.

Kevin Lowery, a Georgia DNR turkey biologist, examined photos of the mounted black turkey and agreed, with some qualifications, that it was a melanistic color phase of the Eastern species. According to NWTF, black is the rarest of the four color mutations, and only one is usually found in 50,000 turkeys.

On a rainy afternoon in late spring, when turkey hunting is at its most difficult, Durrance decided to go hunting. Before leaving his residence, "I stopped by the auto parts store and told Neal I was going hunting and would be back in thirty minutes," Durrance recalled.

Light rain was still falling when he parked his truck on his hunt lease in the next county and immediately spotted six turkeys in the back corner of a clear cut. A random clap of thunder confirmed that a gobbler was in the group.

Knowing he could not call them in the rain, Durrance chose a gutsy strategy...he would mount a frontal assault on the birds by flanking them and charging the flock head on.

Mr. Durrance closed the distance at a dead run, and the startled turkeys flushed...five going in one direction and a single going in another. He downed the single, running gobbler with one shot from his Benelli Vinci 12-gauge.

"When I looked down at the fallen bird, it was black in color, and I had never seen anything like it," he exclaimed.

True to his word, Durrance returned to his hometown within thirty minutes.

Although Durrance was a deer hunter growing up, he switched over to turkey hunting six years ago, primarily at the urging of a friend. Durrance holds two NWTF records in his home county—a gobbler with the longest spur length (1 3/8") and another for longest beard (13"). Both were taken in 2008.

Durrance's approach to turkey hunting is analogous to a QDMA (Quality Deer Management Association) mentality. In other words, he concentrates only on mature gobblers. "It ain't about killing a bird; I want to grow and hunt trophy, dominant strutters," he explained.

He lets Jakes and young birds walk; he uses trail cameras; he scouts year-round, and he roosts gobblers before each morning hunt. Durrance is a "thinking man's" turkey hunter, and man does his philosophy work.

CONFESSIONS OF A TURKEY HUNTER'S WIFE

My wife, Connie, surprised me with this story. I did not ask her to write it. After enduring four decades of frequent absences from home and family on hunting and fishing trips, she earned the right to have her say. With wit and intelligence, she finally reveals what it's like to be a turkey hunter's wife.

On a gloomy February day, I heard the unmistakable sound of yelps and clucks coming from my husband's office. My heart leapt, and I gave a joyous gobble back. I realized spring was close at hand. He is exquisitely tuned to the first signs. His entire life is built around turkey season, no matter which country or state welcomes it first.

He has a Royal Slam. There are six types of turkeys, four in the US and two in Mexico. They are the Eastern, Merriam, Osceola, and Rio Grande in the US, and the Goulds and the Oscellated in Chihuahua and the Yucatan, respectively. All of these fellows are hanging on my walls with the exception of the Oscellated. I've been told he looks like a peacock and doesn't like to fly, so the guides have to hit him with a stick to send him airborne. Therefore, nobody much likes to kill one.

In his early days of turkey hunting, Ken was gone quite a lot during the season. I stayed at a level barely below seething most of the time. I finally realized that my wrath did not deter him one bit because he absolutely loved what

Ken Cook

he was doing. After talking with other turkey widows, some of whom were my aunts and cousins, I found that I was not alone. The advice they gave was to find something I liked as much and pursue it. I did. And I have tried to pass this wisdom on to younger women, but it is rarely well received.

Years of observing turkey hunters have given me hours of laughter and reverence for these men. They hunt relentlessly, sometimes without ever getting a shot. It never dampens their enthusiasm. They prepare constantly off season. They worship at the doors of Bass Pro Shops, Cabela's, and local sporting goods stores.

Apparently, pursuing a turkey requires endless research and study. I was not aware that a turkey has an IQ equal to Einstein and the street smarts of Tony Soprano. All packed into a brain the size of an English pea. I came by this knowledge because I am a voracious reader. Having a huge supply of books on turkeys, I will sometimes reach for one. Tom Kelly has become my favorite turkey author.

Another interesting thing is that a hunter cannot have anything on his body that is shiny or reflective. Turkeys exposed to this have been known to gather their extended families and move to a different zip code. Hunters also have to wear the correct camo. Turkeys are very strict about this. If hunting around Okeechobee, you had better have on the palmetto suit or they won't even look your way. I once came upon four men in my kitchen dressed in this attire and thought a clump of palmettos had suddenly sprung up.

The army camo, tree patterns, and the ghillie suit round out the different looks. This of course includes every piece of gear that is on the hunter. I almost forgot, they blacken their faces and wear hats with veils, as if ready to attend Mass.

A word about the ghillie suit: It is a shaggy-all-over thing and colored just like nature. The only thing I can compare it to is the "Will-o-the Wisp" in Uncle Remus stories. It would scare the wits out of anybody. My five-year-old granddaughter came upon one in Ken's office and has refused to return there. He feels this is a good thing.

Turkey hunters have also perfected the 'freeze' when a gobbler approaches. All movement stops, even if a snake is slithering across their legs or a panther has his forepaws on their shoulders.

It is amazing to me that my sons and nephews, Jared, Scott, Clay, Hank, and Todd, whom to a man loved to sleep late, now rise cheerfully (only Scott and Hank ever rose cheerfully), at 4:30 in the morning, eager to hit the woods. Is all this gear and preparation really necessary? I wonder what the Indians and the early frontiersmen did to prepare for the hunt. I can just hear Jemima Boone saying, "Dan'l, do you want the ghillie sui,t or are you good with the Mossy Oak today?"

My Uncle Butch, a consummate bird hunter, once told me that turkey and grouse hunting approached religion. He called it the "last stage," and it was communing with nature in its purest form. Bless his dear soul. I have finally come to believe this is true.

THE STORY OF JUDAS THE WILD CHICKEN

This will go down as the oddest story I have ever written about turkey hunting. But I have proof and it shall be told.

In the 1960s, the Georgia Game and Fish Commission (at that time) imported Burmese jungle fowl breeding stock in hopes of creating a new game bird species for hunters. The nursery was located at the Bowen's Mill Fish Hatchery, ten miles north of Fitzgerald, Georgia. At some point in the experiment, it was concluded that the probable survival rate of the chickens in the wild was too low due to potential predation, and the experiment was scrubbed.

Apparently, the wild chickens didn't get the e-mail, and they promptly migrated to the town of Fitzgerald, where they took up residence and thrived, merrily scratching up flowerbeds for tasty morsels and disrupting sleeping residents with their incessant crowing.

Though in-town residents soon declared their uninvited guests as pests and nuisances, the wild chickens proved to be a tourism boon for the City of Fitzgerald. Tim Anderson, Editor and Publisher of the *Fitzgerald Herald-Leader*, told me that their recent seventeenth annual Wild Chicken Festival drew ten to fifteen thousand visitors and earned yet another feather in the cap of the local Jaycees, who host the popular event.

Trey, and his father are turkey-hunting partners of some renown, and they have a hunting lease some five to ten miles east of Fitzgerald. While scouting for deer in the fall of 2012, they noticed something other than deer on their trail camera photos. Having firsthand knowledge of what a wild chicken looks like, they made a positive ID. The colorful rooster was indeed a wild chicken, far removed from his normal habitat and mingling with a flock of wild turkeys.

Throughout deer season and into the spring gobbler season of 2013, Trey's father threatened to dispatch the noisy rooster, but Trey convinced his dad to leave him be. This later proved to be a wise decision.

You see, the wild chicken had been accepted by the wild turkeys on the property and would presumably roost with the turkeys, mingle, travel, and feed with them. But as was his genetic directive, the chicken would crow at all hours of the night and also at the appointed time of daybreak when turkeys usually arise.

The hunting buddies smartly noted that when the chicken crowed at first light, the wild turkeys would gobble in response [as hunters know, this is called involuntary "shock gobbling"]. They also observed that when they used their turkey calls, the chicken would fly down and come to their setup from which they were calling. And, you guessed it, the turkeys would mimic the rooster, fly down, and join him.

Trey named the wild chicken "Judas" because his crowing would cause the turkeys to gobble, thus revealing their roosting location, which is always kept secret. And when Judas flew down and came to their calling, he lured the turkeys to follow him like a modern day Pied Piper, straight into the sights of the hunter's Browning shotguns.

Trey and his dad were out early on their lease on March 22, opening day of the 2014 spring turkey season. But Judas didn't crow that morning. Nor did he make an appearance. Still, the father-son team managed to call in several gobblers without Judas, and Trey flattened two birds with one shot and his dad took a third gobbler.

Maybe I can trap-and-transfer a wild chicken rooster and take him to my hunting grounds. I could sure use his help.

JUST SHOOT!

For the past four spring turkey seasons, I have been unalterably perched on the horns of a dilemma. And it's hurting my pride and my reputation as a decent turkey hunter. I need professional help, which is why I decided to go public with this story.

I took my first wild turkey in Alabama in 1990 and immediately contracted what Ben Lee called the "turkey disease." For the next ten years, I chased and killed wild turkeys in Texas, Florida, Arizona, and Mexico. At the end of the decade, turkey parts (tail fan, spurs, and beard) from five different subspecies hung on my den wall. Though I never registered the kills with the NWTF, this feat qualified me for a Royal Slam.

Although the "fever" never broke afterwards, I hit the wall in 2011 and didn't bag a turkey. I had plenty of good excuses for not taking one, but the 2012 season produced the same result—no turkey. In 2013, I missed a Missouri tom I should have killed. Mentally, I hit the bottom of the barrel. If this jinx was real, I told myself, it had to end. I needed redemption, and it had to come in the 2014 season.

My plan for redemption involved enlisting the aid of some of the best turkey hunters in Georgia and Missouri. Mr. Durrance of South Georgia did all he could, and the Missouri contingent—Gary, Bob, and Tim—pulled out all the stops to help bandage my wounded pride. All of these pro hunters produced two, reasonably good opportunities for me to pull the trigger on a bird and I failed to do so.

I returned to Georgia down trodden and feeling defeated. I entertained thoughts of retiring from turkey hunting and passing my gear down to my sons. Stalking my thoughts were visions of a longbeard loping across a plowed field thirty-five yards in front of me and a strutting gobbler within twenty-five yards who spooked, putted, and was quickly downed by one of the Schrages. Painful memories.

In both cases, I never fully mounted my shotgun and took the shots that had been graciously presented to me. Though somewhat chancy, both were makeable.

It is customary for all turkey hunters to analyze and continuously replay a kill or a missed bird. And that is what I did. The answer to my analytical journey came surprisingly quickly. I had developed a phobia, of sorts, of shooting and missing (or wounding) a bird, and this feeling had been languishing in the back of my mind since 2013, when I shot and missed a tom. I reasoned that I had been waiting for the "perfect shot," and turkeys never give you that edge.

Though I remain scoreless after four seasons, I now have a solution to my phobia and a renewed vigor about turkey hunting. When your experience tells you a shot is makeable, JUST SHOOT!

THE EASTER SNAP IS NO MATCH FOR THE BIRDS AND BEES.

First Place in Newspaper Writing,
Georgia Outdoor Writers Association, 2014

On the third day of Georgia's spring 2013 turkey season, I sat huddled under a red cedar tree on the edge of a bright green cow pasture. Not a cloud in the sky. Winds were howling and buffeted me with gusts topping forty miles per hour.

I watched apprehensively as my hen decoy, twenty yards beyond, spun like a top on its stake, and would soon come to rest in an unnatural position that the dumbest of turkeys would not have dared to approach. The hood of my camo jacket was cinched so tight, I couldn't have heard a gobble if the bird's beak had been resting on my shoulder.

Sure enough, the Easter Snap collided head on with this year's Georgia turkey season opener. And it's still hanging around. My grandpa used the term "Easter Snap" to describe an inhospitable weather phenomenon that, without warning, usually visits just when we think winter has ended. Old timers were never fooled into planting until the Easter Snap had passed, no matter how many redbuds and dogwoods were budding or in bloom.

Turkey mating behavior is triggered biologically by continuously warming days and cool nights. Wind, rain, and cold (or any combination thereof) has a way of temporarily stalling gobbling, breeding, and turning hunter expressions into frowns. So it was that the Easter Snap dropped in on us on opening weekend and squashed hunting opportunities faster than a road killed possum.

Ken Cook

Another thing we learned this year is that hunters can't outrun the Easter Snap. We traveled to Kentucky and Missouri hoping to get a jump on the Easter Snap, but the Easter Snap yields no quarter to turkey hunters. Intermittent warm, sunny days are normal during an Easter Snap, and there were enough of them to permit some hunting, at least in Southern Kentucky.

In the hilly ground around Todd County, Kentucky, my son downed a fine twenty-five-pound bird after escaping detection from three curious hens and watching the boss gobbler win a challenge match with a sub-dominant tom. My son ended the afternoon matinee with a load of 12-gauge, three-inch magnum Hevi-Shot loads.

The five-day weather forecast for Northeastern Missouri, my personal favorite for turkey hunting, did not look good on arrival for our three-day hunt. We correctly surmised that the Easter Snap was revving its engines at the starting line, but we still hunted the first afternoon and the following morning.

Yours truly called in a young gobbler but rushed the shot and missed the bird. Patience is a compulsory turkey hunting virtue that seems to be evaporating in concert with my age.

Before torrential rains brought our Missouri hunt to a close, I witnessed a sight that was almost as dramatic as killing a three-year tom. Four gobblers and nine hens flew down from their roost into a field not more than fifty yards in front of my setup.

The nine hens surrounded my hen decoy, putting an invisible wedge between my decoy and their gobblers. Throwing every seductive call in my backpack at the gobblers proved to be in vain. The hens slowly led the toms over the hill and out of sight.

The Easter Snap is a powerful phenomenon, but no match for the birds and bees

Ken Cook

Bobwhite
QUAIL

WILL BOBWHITES EVER
MAKE A COMEBACK?

I f you're in my age group (seventy plus) and were raised in the rural south, fond memories of quail hunting are forever etched in your mind. I deeply miss the camaraderie, great dog work, and the heart-stopping flush of a wild covey.

My last encounter with wild quail was in Southern Illinois in the mid-1980s. Since then, it has been preserve shooting of pen-raised birds offered by commercial outfitters. This isn't the same, but it has served as an adequate tonic for what ails chronic quail hunters who miss the good old days.

Restoration of the American Wild Turkey by the National Wild Turkey Federation has kept alive my dream that I may one day witness the return of viable populations of bobwhites in their natural, geographic range. And I have begun to see some sunlight at the end of this long, dark tunnel.

Here is what I found out from digging into the literature and talking with John Doty, Communications Director of the National Bobwhite Conservation Initiative (NBCI), the lead dog in the quail restoration effort. NBCI is based in Knoxville, Tennessee at the University of Tennessee's Institute of Agriculture.

Any sportsman remotely conversant in species conservation realizes that a gargantuan project like bobwhite restoration requires enabling legislation, a strong coalition of state and federal agencies and conservation groups, funding, research and testing, planning, and implementation. These

Ken Cook

activities and more have been going on since 2002 and will continue to accelerate the momentum now taking place.

Currently there are twenty-five states cooperating in this overall initiative, and biologists have classified 195 million acres as having "medium to high" potential for bobwhite conservation. Prescribed burning and field/field-edge management are two of the pressing requirements in the overall conservation plan.

Georgia, where quail was once king, has been at the forefront of the habitat enhancement initiative. Restoration efforts have now been extended to sixty-eight Upper Coastal Plain counties where science shows the potential for improvement is greatest.

Has there been significant progress to date? You bet. We now know what to do, where to do it, and the probability of success from various on-the-ground endeavors. And the beneficiaries from these conservation efforts will not only be bobwhites, but turkeys, songbirds, and other species that can use a boost.

John Doty told me that "broad scale, range-wide restoration of bobwhites" remains a steep mountain to scale, but there are lots of focal-point geographies in the twenty-five states that are already experiencing increases in bobwhite populations.

If you are a landowner or tree farmer and relish the idea of once again hearing the shrill whistle of the bobwhite and just seeing these birds on your property, here are two things I urge you to do: First, go to www.bringbackbob-whites.org to learn more about what NBCI partners are doing and what videos and literature are available for you to read. If so moved, get on the bandwagon and become engaged. Second, contact a Georgia Wildlife Resources

Division (WRD) biologist and tell him you are interested in managing your property for quail. They can assess your property and tell you about financial incentives that may help optimize quail habitat.

Ken Cook

A BOBWHITE SAFARI

I t's ironic how perception and reality can be so close at times and so far apart at others.

For example, my perception of Safari Club International (SCI) was an organization comprised solely of well-heeled captains of industry, toting $20,000 big-bore rifles, traveling the world in search of exotic big game animals to populate their immense trophy rooms.

Boy, was I misinformed and judgmental. My perception shift began after I interviewed and wrote a newspaper column about a Georgia small business owner who had taken three African safaris and was planning his fourth.

About a year later, I wrote a second column about an elementary school teacher, raised in a non-hunting household, who became a huntress under the tutelage of her husband. They took an African safari, and she harvested several animals. She is now witnessing for hunting and SCI.

For me, perception and reality finally merged at the Epic Game Fair near Atlanta last fall. There, I spent some time at the SCI booth and talked briefly with Joe Hosmer. I joined the ranks on the spot and later linked up with the Atlanta chapter.

SCI is an organization whose mission is to protect the freedom to hunt and promote wildlife conservation worldwide. There are over 50,000 members and 190 local chapters. The organization has its own scoring system and Record Book; produces the largest convention for hunters; funds outdoor educational programs, humanitarian services and scholarships.

I didn't wait long to meet some SCI members in person. Steven Bender of the Atlanta chapter organized a weekend quail hunt at Southern Woods Plantation near Sylvester, Georgia, a 2,500-acre bobwhite quail preserve I had previously hunted. Seven SCI members showed up for the hunt.

Doubts and questions filled my blaze orange ball cap. Would these guys accept me? Would I fit in? Would I be ashamed of my shotgun and hunting attire? Was it safe for four guys to hunt next to each other? Are these hunters crack shots on bobwhites?

By the third covey rise, all apprehensions dissipated. I was now just part of a four-man hunting squad that, to a man, was very social, hunted safely, missed easy shots, made tough shots, and enjoyed excellent work by English pointers and English cocker spaniel flushing dogs. Nothing short of a memorable day afield with some great guys and upland bird hunters.

Over cocktails before dinner, one of our hunters, a corporate pilot who has flown jets to 105 countries, showed me photos of a magnificent, record-book lion he took in the Kalahari Desert on his last African safari (he has taken four trips). I was not only enthralled by his story, but also impressed by his views on conservation and the singular beauty of Africa and its big game animals.

As all true hunting sportsmen and conservationists should, I genuinely support the Safari Club's mission and its advocacy programs. As for whether I'll someday take an African safari, perception is now closing in on reality.

THE MIGHTY BOBWHITE

As a hunter and outdoor writer, I am continually amazed at the attention, interest, and money leveled at a five-ounce game bird with a one-year lifespan, commonly known as the bobwhite quail.

Once found in thirty states, the species has been in decline since the early 1900s and, as late as 1966, was tracked by game biologists as disappearing at the rate of three percent annually. Yet Mr. Bob still holds the official title of Georgia's State Game Bird, and Georgia wing shooters proudly cling to the claim, "Quail Capital of the US"

Unless you are long in the tooth and faintly recall the good old days of hunting wild quail (as I do), the principal choice for most hunters today is booking a guided hunt at a commercial hunting lodge and shooting pen-raised birds. Mind you, this is not a disparaging remark, because most commercial operations today offer quality quail hunting and first-class food and lodging.

For the past two years, members of the Atlanta Chapter of Safari Club International have traveled to Southern Woods Plantation near Sylvester, Georgia, in Worth County for the club's annual, plantation-style quail hunt.

This year, twelve SCI members made the trip, and I hunted with three of them. Mr. Rodgers, our experienced guide, and several braces of lean pointers were able to provide two challenging half-days of bird shooting.

In many ways, our experience at Southern Woods far exceeds the quail hunts of yesteryear. Stately pines, native wiregrass, and broomsedge dominate the habitat. We were comfortably transported from area to area in a jeep-drawn hunt trailer, and fresh dogs were released at each stop. Despite what you may have heard, flight-conditioned, pen-raised birds don't allow mulligans.

Bird hunting is as much a social affair as it is a shooting experience, and Southern Woods excels at providing after-the-hunt opportunities to make new friends over a favorite beverage and a good southern meal. And when the day is done, overnight lodgers walk to their rooms with smiles on their faces.

Safari Club members, for the most part, are inveterate, well-traveled hunters who pursue dangerous game on several continents. With so many options at their disposal, why, I wondered, would these sportsmen prefer to hunt bobwhite quail over other forms of wing shooting? There are a few reasons:

- Two gun dogs locked on point is guaranteed to send adrenaline coursing through a hunter's body as he moves in toward the explosive flush;
- Quail hunting provides the rare opportunity to take a beloved, antique shotgun to the field and resurrect memories;
- Whether pen-raised or wild birds, quail hunting is both challenging and humbling shooting for the best of hunters;
- Whether you only read about it or actually experienced it, bird hunting is a vivid and nostalgic connection to hunting's glory days;
- Quail hunting is possibly the most social type of hunting that exists today; and

- As table fare, quail has no equal among upland game birds.

So, what's your reason for not planning and booking a bobwhite quail hunt this season?

Duck
HUNTING

JUST DUCKY

L iving over two hundred miles from a major waterfowl flyway makes for slim pickings if you enjoy duck and goose hunting. Most Georgia waterfowl hunters are pretty much left with a choice of large lakes with some cover, beaver ponds, or flooded acorn flats off the main stem of a river.

None of these duck havens are easy to locate, access is usually restricted, and busting brush in the dark (in waders) is nothing short of a waltz between your heart and the grim reaper.

Duck hunters are a hearty, indomitable group, however. Imagine getting up at 3:00 in the morning, driving to a secluded area, donning thirty-five pounds of equipment (waders, gun, shells, decoys, and layers of camo clothing), crashing through thick brush with only the aid of a pencil-thin flashlight, and praying there are no leaks in your waders as you embark into the water.

If this description sounds worse than water boarding, wait. There's more. Rain, sleet, and freezing temperatures keep most hunters at home in bed. Not duck hunters. Ducks relish nasty weather, and so do the duck hunters who pursue them

The distance from the bank to your makeshift duck blind in the water is a hold-your-breath shuffle, hoping you won't step into a beaver run or trip over a sunken log. Both hazards will "float your hat" as they say.

The grand finale of these duck hunting excursions is usually thirty to forty minutes of frenzied shooting, and then the hunt is over. Your energy level gauge is now flashing red, and you wince at the thought of having to retrace your steps back through the water and brush to the truck.

Recently, I found out firsthand that I should hang up my waders and leave this type of duck hunting to those between the ages of thirty and fifty—an age group I am no longer a part of. But refusing an invitation to go duck hunting is hard for an old duck hunter still harboring memories of past shoots. So, I accepted the invitation and even practiced putting on a pair of borrowed, insulated neoprene waders the night before. I was puzzled by my partner's parting comment, "And don't forget to bring a walking staff taller than your head."

I was a trooper until I stepped into the chocolate-colored water strewn with floating debris and lost visual contact with the boots on my waders. The water got deeper, and I could feel a muddy bottom laden with limbs and logs. "Now this is the only hard part; we now have to traverse an eighteen-inch manmade walkway over the deepest water to get to our blind," they told me.

With age and the infirmities that accompany it, I said, "I don't think I can make this walk, fellas, and I don't feel like taking a dunking in forty-seven degree water; I'll just take a position on the bank." With that, they walked on and I headed for the bank.

Sunrise brought forth a postcard morning and a noisy serenade of wild turkeys leaving their roosts. Several flocks of wood ducks flew over the duck hole, and the guys connected with two of them. In my case, wisdom and a good decision allowed me to connect with another memorable outing in the great outdoors.

THE DUCKS AND JUDGES
ANSWERED CHAD'S CALLS

Although the only body of duck water nearby was the Ocmulgee River, the Macon, Georgia, Centreplex on a hot July afternoon seemed an unlikely time and place to be calling in ducks. Not so for the fifteen Georgians competing for the 2011 Georgia State Duck Calling Championship.

Three rounds of eliminations were necessary before Mr. Poole, aged thirty-seven, was finally declared the winner. He took home a large trophy, $300 in prize money, and an invitation to the World Championship calling contest in Stuttgart, Arkansas, in November.

Duck calling contests are serious business, and this wasn't Mr. Poole's first rodeo. He had previously competed in a number of calling contests in other states, capturing the 2009 Georgia Championship and third place in the 2004 Georgia contest.

The five judges for this event came from as far away as Maryland and Arkansas. Hidden from the judge's view, each caller, who is identified by number rather than name, is required to blow a routine that includes four duck calls—hail call, meeting/greeting call, feeding call, and a come-back call. Contestants are allotted ninety seconds to blow their routine in each round.

Although the calls are technically the same, the interpretations, volume, timing, and inflections are audibly different. These are the nuances that judges, all of whom are seasoned duck callers and competitors themselves, have a finely tuned ear for.

Duck calling competitors don't make it this far without a supportive family and colleagues in the call making and contest calling business. Mr. Poole credits a friend with showing him how to blow a routine, and two owners of Refuge Calls pledged their continuing support.

Poole was first a dedicated duck hunter before he became interested in contest calling. "For me, calling competitions gave me an opportunity to make new friends, extend the duck season, and to get better at what I love to do," he said with pride.

The World Championship in Stuttgart in November, the granddaddy of all duck calling competitions, is squarely in Mr. Poole's sights. His training routine will be intense, including participating in a few nonsanctioned events and daily practice sessions. These include breaking his routine into sections, practicing them over and over, audio recording each one, and putting them all back together. The recordings are then e-mailed to his supporters for serious critique.

Until a contest caller dons the "Green Jacket," so to speak, the money needed to travel and compete is self-funded. Although Refuge Calls pays his entry fee to the World competition, and Hevi-Shot and Rig'Em Right hunting accessories provide free product, it's a long, uphill climb to the top where the real sponsor money lies.

Poole's "Stradivarius" is a Refuge Call, and the model is "The Ticket." He moved on from the Georgia state championship to the World Championship in Stuttgart with high hopes, but failed to win.

Ken Cook

Mourning
DOVES

THE SOUND OF A MILLION WING BEATS

If there is one thing wing shooters can agree on, it's a dove shooting trip to La Volanta Lodge in the Cordoba Province of Argentina, the dove capital of the world. It was unquestionably the trip of a lifetime and another check-off on my "bucket list."

Though getting there was grueling, the shooting was unparalleled. I had joined a group of five expert shotgunners who, to a man, said they saw more doves on the first day than they had seen in their lifetime. And these were wing shooters over the age of fifty.

Cordoba Province is home to an estimated thirty million doves. They feed, roost, and breed in an agricultural area densely populated with rich grain crops—sorghum, milo, corn, wheat, soybeans, and sunflower. The birds do not migrate, and shooting is year-round.

The primary subspecies of dove in the area is the eared dove, a smallish dove (four ounces) with a black hash mark under each eye and subtle gold hash marks down its neck. What they lack in size, they make up with speed, keen eyesight, instant flaring, and enormous flocks that challenge hunters.

The nine-year-old La Volanta Dove Hunting Lodge has cornered the market on doves, leasing over 5,000 acres of prime shooting habitat for its guests. Morning shoots took place in an unharvested grain sorghum field, and afternoon shoots were along treelined hedgerows adjacent to harvested fields. Guests were ferried to shooting areas

Ken Cook

in a van and travel time was never over fifteen to twenty minutes.

Spacious, immaculate accommodations with tile floors and large baths welcome tired hunters after a day in the fields. Meals are hearty, creatively prepared, and served with a selection of fine Argentinian wines. Argentinian beef is present at almost every meal. As you might also expect, service is impeccable.

La Volanta welcomes women and kids, as well as male sportsmen. While we were there, guests included two couples, two grandfathers and two boys aged eleven and twelve. Shooters can bring their own shotguns, but the lodge provides reliable and tested Beretta 20-gauge semi-auto shotguns for rental. Fiocchi shot shells are the outfitter's preference.

A "Bird Boy" is assigned to each hunter and remains with them throughout the trip. These men, including one woman, make their livelihood taking care of the shooters' needs while in the field. Aside from improving my shooting percentage each time I went out, the number of shooting opportunities is so great, that it is easy to self-correct any nagging shooting problems.

If you decide to go, and I heartily recommend it, here are some helpful hints: Talk with hunters who have previously traveled there; plan your flight through Santiago, Chile; camouflage is helpful but not mandatory; take along sunscreen and insect repellant; purchase an Evoshield padded shooting shirt; rent your shotgun from the outfitter; and check the five-day weather forecast. NWTF fundraising banquets are a good place to purchase a group trip.

BELLWETHER OF THE FALL
HUNTING SEASON

Unless you're a hunter or from a hunting family, you might wonder how a five-ounce game bird could ignite a statewide celebration on the first weekend in September. Well, welcome to the opening day of dove season in Georgia and the symbolic start of the fall hunting season.

Opening-day dove shoots have evolved into homecoming events, partly because hunters have been idle for fifteen weeks and partly because they've missed being outdoors with friends and family. These gatherings are as much social affairs and reunions as they are hunting outings.

Although the key ingredients of an opening day shoot may vary, they almost always include an early lunch of slow-cooked pork barbeque, Brunswick stew, coleslaw, potato salad, and cold beverages prior to the legal start of noon shooting. Cooking, eating, and socializing take place under a large, covered pavilion cooled by circulating fans. For those who want a football aperitif, college games are getting underway on a big screen TV.

I have attended many opening-day events over the years, but this year was a chart topper. Mr. Bloodworth of Tift County, Georgia, was our host and hunt master. Thirty-three years of practice have put him in the "professional" category. Not only does he know how to prepare fields that attract doves, but our host slow-smokes ham and sausage so loaded with flavor you'll come back for third helpings. His Brunswick stew is as authentic as I have ever tasted.

Social time and food are important but a successful dove shoot is consummated on the field. Guests naturally want to see a lot of birds and have opportunities to limit out. Bloodworth excels at managing multiple fields, overseeing crop harvesting, and scheduling shooting days and hours so that he can host good dove shoots throughout the three split seasons and into January.

When I asked our host if there were plenty of doves using the fields we would be shooting, he smiled and said, "There are so many birds, they have to take shifts feeding." He wasn't wrong.

On opening day, our group of twenty-five shot over a sixteen-acre sunflower field. On a mourning dove's menu, sunflowers rank a close second to peanuts, which had not been harvested at the time we shot. During our three-hour shoot, there was not a single minute when birds were not entering or exiting the field. Our host estimated several thousand doves had been feeding in this field in the days leading up to opening day.

Tired, sweaty, and satisfied, the shooters returned to the barn and gathered in small groups to replay their best shots and accept some ragging for their misses. More food was set out, kids and their dads played games, and football fans caught up on all the scores. It was as close to a perfect opening day as I can remember.

MY "VIRTUAL" OPENING
DAY DOVE SHOOT

My favorite day of the year is the opening day of dove season. It sends a loud and clear signal to Georgia hunters that we can now pick up where we left off last May and start hunting once again.

But the opening day of dove season is far more than just the ceremonial beginning of a new hunting year. It's an annual one-day affair marked by pulled-pork barbeque, young dog breeds whose nervous owners pray their pups will find and retrieve a downed bird, and a sunflower field crowded with hunters young and old whose faces are turned skyward searching for the first flight of zigzagging, winged speedsters adept at avoiding poorly-placed shots. Hunters swat gnats and mosquitos, busily wipe sweat from their brows, and rationalize loudly their miscues. That's the way it is in the dove field on opening afternoon.

This year, I will not be joining this traditional fandangle. No one invited me to come and shoot with them. And I can't spare $125 for a paid shoot with fifty percent odds that birds will show up. So I will have to enjoy a shoot vicariously, or as they say in the high-tech business, "A virtual, opening day dove shoot."

There are several steps I can take to enjoy a virtual dove shoot this Saturday afternoon, September 6. Here are the ways I've come up with:

- Take my over/under Browning 12-gauge from its case after breakfast and clean it to a fair-the-well.
- Make sure I have four boxes of field load shells and several choke tubes.
- Find my dove bucket with the swivel top; pack insect repellant, sunscreen, and a twelve-pack of bottled water. And don't forget Power Bars to snack on.
- Pull from the back of the closet my lightweight camo pants, shirt, cap, gloves, facemask, and high-top boots.
- Insert a DVD in the TV set and watch a real live dove shoot between chores. Nothing is as motivational as a hunting/shooting video to recall the basics of leading the bird and locating the best set up positions in a dove field.
- Take a short nap in the backyard hammock to renew my strength and stamina before leaving for the dove field.
- Fall fast asleep dreaming about the Argentina dove shoot two years ago when five hundred downed birds put me in last place among our group of shooters. And we left the harvested cornfield with doves still obscuring the sunset and lighting in the trees along the hedgerow I just left.
- Awaken from my nap and rush inside to play an Xbox game on bird shooting. Got my fifteen-bird limit in no time at all.

The next thing I know, my wife yells from the kitchen, "Put all that hunting gear away and come to supper; we're having country fried steak and lima beans tonight."

You can sure build up a hearty appetite on an opening-day dove shoot—real or imagined.

Part V:

THE INHABITANTS

Hats Off To VENOMOUS SNAKES

RATTLESNAKES GET A BUM RAP

Being a sportsman and descendant of pine stumpers and loggers, I have had many encounters with poisonous snakes. While most were unpleasant, I don't harbor a paralyzing fear of snakes. Their bite will kill you even though you're five times more likely to succumb to a lightning strike.

It's not easy being a rattlesnake. Like the hash brown options at the local all-night diner, rattlesnakes have been scattered, smothered, covered, chunked, diced, topped, and peppered. With scant knowledge of the good deeds they do, or the medical benefits derived from their venom, it seems that most outdoor enthusiasts still cling to the old adage, "the only good snake is a dead snake."

I recently joined a friend, Scott Revell, on a March rattlesnake hunt on my nephew's wooded South Georgia farm. He is a veteran snake hunter whose captures are sold alive and healthy to a venom extracting facility in Alabama.

Commercial facilities like this one "milk" the snakes, remove impurities, and freeze-dry the liquid venom into a powder form. Fully processed venom is then stored and sold to research labs, universities, and pharmaceutical companies. While in their care, snakes are fed, cared for, and often give birth in captivity.

Eastern diamondback rattlers, the largest and most prevalent of the cold-blooded species in South Georgia, like to pass the winter months underground in gopher tortoise burrows. They hibernate in winter, breed in the spring, and after a ninety-day gestation, give birth in the fall to clutches of five to twelve live juveniles. A rattler's life span is ten to twenty years.

The gopher tortoise is an endangered species, and gasoline is no longer used (nor is legal) in coaxing rattlesnakes from their holes. Today, tools of the trade include a "listening tube," a flexible pipe inserted into the hole to listen for rattling; a shovel to enlarge the hole's opening; a flashlight to help locate the snake inside the hole; a crooked stick to pull the snake from the burrow; and a noose stick to lift and place the snake in a secure holding box.

Walking in snake chaps through briars and undergrowth for several hours is physically taxing, aside from the potential danger in locating and capturing a poisonous snake. Scott and I hunted for three hours before he dialed up a nice diamondback and safely retrieved him from a gopher hole.

Two of the earliest uses of rattlesnake venom were in the manufacture of antivenom for human snakebites and also production of a serum designed to immunize horses. Today, medical research has significantly expanded the curative powers locked inside snake venom. Rattlesnake venom is used in the drug Byetta to treat Type 2 diabetes, as well as in blood-thinning drugs and medications treating high blood pressure.

You may not want to drop a "thank you" note in a gopher tortoise burrow, but give rattlesnakes their space and spare their lives. Their numbers are declining, and their venom may someday be used to lengthen your time on this planet.

Deer
HUNTING

QDMA: THE DEER HUNTER'S FRIEND

For years, I observed the blaze orange signs hanging from cabled and gated entry roads to woodland properties without really knowing what they stood for. Compounding my ignorance was the fact that the Quality Deer Management Association (QDMA) is headquartered in my hometown of Athens.

Ignorance and procrastination can only last so long, especially when it's leveled at an outdoor writer. This year, QDMA held its 2013 National Convention in Athens, and I was dead set on being there to learn and participate in the sessions.

QDMA, a nonprofit organization, is twenty-five years old this year, and though its record of accomplishments are now many, it was a "long row to hoe" for founder Joe Hamilton of South Carolina in the early years.

Imagine trying to convince landowners, hunt clubs, and deer hunters that there is a better way to manage their deer herd, improve habitat, conserve natural resources, and grow healthy deer.

The deer hunting culture and practice in my early years was based on, "shoot anything with horns" and "let all does walk." That philosophy was so deeply ingrained in the minds of deer hunters that it might as well have been tattooed on their shooting hands. It never occurred to members of our hunt club why the buck to doe ratio was way out of whack, and few mature, well-antlered bucks were ever seen, much less harvested.

The birthplace of QDM was actually in Texas around 1960. Two wildlife biologists began formulating their novel ideas on deer management. Their concepts and practices later surfaced in a book titled, "Producing Quality Whitetails," published in 1975. Their methods spread slowly into other parts of the whitetail's range and is now considered the most desirable and biologically sound deer-management approach for today's herds.

The four building blocks of QDM are herd management, habitat management, hunter management, and herd monitoring. While there is not enough space in this column to define and illuminate what each building block includes, QDM is essentially a management strategy that produces healthy deer herds with balanced adult-sex ratios and improved buck-age structures.

To be sure, QDM is not for every landowner or hunt club. Generally, about 2,000 plus acres are needed to make the program work, although a group of individual property owners can form a cooperative and satisfy contiguous acreage guidelines.

A firm commitment by landowners and hunters to the philosophy and practices is perhaps the most important link in the chain. Preparing habitat will require dollars and man-hours; gathering and recording harvest data takes time and effort; and patience and resolve are needed to stay connected to the program, knowing it may be several years before optimum results are achieved.

WHO YOU GONNA CALL?

If you hunt deer long enough and hard enough, you'll eventually wound a big-rack buck and be unable to find him. It happens to the best of hunters and marksmen. A hunter's first reaction is to spend countless hours trying to find or follow a faint blood trail. The second is to enlist the aid of a hound, anybody's hound, to look for the deer. The last reaction should be your first one, and that is to call a recovery dog specialist whose dogs are trained to blood-track wounded deer.

Randy Vick is one of the best at finding wounded animals for hunters. Last deer season, Randy took seventy calls from clients. From this number, he confirmed five missed shots on deer, blood-trailed sixty-five, and retrieved twenty-nine bucks. Without his expert assistance, these big-rack bucks (one of whom scored 158) would have otherwise been left to the coyotes and vultures.

Many deer hunters don't realize the instinctive tricks a wounded buck can play on a hunter or tracking dog to escape capture. Randy has seen them backtrack up to four hundred yards and also run in wide circles or a cloverleaf pattern. Many times, he has trailed them across streams and big rivers. He's even seen them go to water and leave it.

Even when seriously wounded, whitetail deer summon up deep energy reserves. Wounded bucks will sometimes seek out healthy deer to run with and disguise their route of flight. "I can also confirm that a three-legged deer can outswim a dog in a big river," Randy said.

Randy is part of an elite group of recovery dog owners belonging to the United Blood Trackers organization. He estimates that there are about fifty members in Georgia and two hundred nationwide. Deer and hog hunting with dogs occupied much of Randy's adult life before he started doing game recovery about fifteen years ago.

Recovery dogs are instinctive scent trailers but have to be taught to pick up the scent of blood. There are also training techniques to ensure that the dog will stay on the trail of a wounded deer even though the dog may cross the path of a live, healthy deer. Breeds that Randy prefers are a bloodhound/Catahoula cross, half beagle/half black 'n tan, Kemmer stock mountain cur, and a Bavarian mountain bloodhound.

Working like a forensic specialist, Randy asks a lot of questions when a hunter calls and also when Randy reaches the hunting site. These questions reveal a lot about what he's up against. The color of the blood, color of hair found, deer's reaction to the shot, length of time since the shot, property lines, presence of nearby water, good directions to the hunters, and confirmation that the hunters are legal, are his key questions.

Unknowingly, hunters sometimes compromise a site with too many people walking around or searching on four-wheelers. Exhaust fumes are one of the worst barriers facing trailing dogs.

Randy's work occasionally reveals some incredible stories. Old Bob, a beagle/treeing walker cross, now deceased, was one of the best he ever owned. Bob once trailed a wounded deer for twelve hours, took a three-hour break, returned at daylight, and tracked twelve more hours. Although Bob almost touched the deer four times and covered a mile without blood, the deer was never recovered.

Recovery dog owners set their own fees, but Randy, who takes calls within a one-hundred-mile radius of his home, only asks for his gas money and tips. "I don't want money to stand in the way of leaving a wounded deer in the field," he said.

Ken Cook

BUCK RUT FEVER

Unless a hunter calls me real soon about downing a trophy buck, this column will be my annual deer story for the 2011–2012 season. While everything in this story is true, it's actually a lighthearted spoof, and faces and names were masked to preserve anonymity and respectability

The "deer rut" is a two- to four-week period, which usually falls in November in Georgia, and it is the time when nature signals the deer population that it's time to mate. It's also the time when, in pursuit of their mandate, male deer throw caution to the wind, commit irrevocable errors, and give hunters their best opportunity for a shot.

Anonymous Ed is a hardworking salesman who loves his job, his family, and deer hunting but has never been able to balance all three. When he's engaged in one, he is guilt-ridden about neglecting the other two. His family doesn't understand (or care) about his passion for deer hunting and wishes he would spend more time at home. It's a classic conflict rarely discussed outside the confines of the family TV room.

Ed was willing to give up most of his deer season, but he drew the line on the rut. No way was he going to sit at home and miss the best days of the deer season.

By the time firearm season arrived, Ed was a wreck—physically and mentally. He no longer needed nail clippers because he had bitten them off, and sound sleep was only induced by his new prescription of Lunesta. His wife was asking why he seemed so distant, and his kids had taken a hiatus on asking why they couldn't go to Chuck E. Cheese for pizza and games.

Finally, the postman brought relief—*Georgia Outdoor News*'s Deer Hunting Special issue had arrived. Ed tore through the pages to find the magazine's county-by-county state map to the Peak of the Rut. The dates were now official. It was a eureka moment for Ed. His blood pressure rose, his eyes narrowed, and sweat beaded on his forehead—telltale symptoms of buck rut fever and Ed sprang into action.

That night he took his family to dinner, ordered a Super Colossal pizza, and told them he would be going deer hunting. The rut was underway on his hunt lease. His announcement met with eye rolls but, as expected, no audible response.

It was the busy season at work, and the most time Ed could squeeze from his calendar was two hunt days. On the day he left for the hunt camp, the weather took an ominous turn upward into the eighties, a sure sign that the rut would slow down. Still, Ed arrived in time to climb into his tree stand and catch the last two hours of daylight. Not a sign of a deer.

The next day brought more of the same. Though he hunted most of the daylight hours, Ed saw only two does, one being chased by a buck. The deer were out of range and moving too fast for a sure shot. Though Ed's confidence was flagging, he reminded himself that when a hunt's duration is only two days, tons of luck are needed.

On the last morning before he packed for home, a small spike buck tiptoed quietly into a food plot 110 yards from Ed's stand. Ed studied the animal carefully. Though his rack placed him in the junior category, the deer was

Ken Cook

a legal buck and Ed was in urgent need of an antidote for his raging buck rut fever. BOOM!

Squirrel
HUNTING

HUNTING SMALL GAME WITH RAPTORS

here was no click of a safety or report from a hunting rifle. Only a powerful downdraft of air beneath the wings of a magnificent bird leaving his perch on a falconer's glove. A squirrel hunt in the hardwood forests of Northeast Georgia was on, and the weapon of choice was a red-tailed hawk named Heath.

Hunting with trained birds of prey or raptors has been going on for thousands of years in all corners of the world. Though the sport of falconry got started in this country in the early 1900s, it is still not well known, nor does it have a large following, a fact partly attributable to a rigorous state and federal licensing process and a two-year apprenticeship. Falconry is arguably the most highly regulated of all hunting sports.

The bond and hunting relationship between a falconer and his bird is not unlike imprinting between animals and their newborns. Most falconers trap their birds in the wild and begin a period of patient, eye-to-eye training and frequent hunting trials. Though the relationship strengthens over time, falconers always know their birds might someday fly away and never return.

According to the DNR, raptors in Georgia constitute about eight percent of all state birds. Primarily, eagles, falcons, hawks, and owls make up the category. While red-tailed hawks, red-shouldered hawks, and American kestrels (sparrow hawks) are available to falconers, the workhorse of the group in the southeast is the red-tailed species. Birds of prey are flesh-eating predators with powerful, oversized talons that grab, hold, and kill their quarry, and long, curved beaks for piercing and tearing flesh.

Watching a red-tailed hawk hunt squirrels is an experience somewhere between an airshow and a Keystone Cops episode. When the quarry is sighted, the falconer releases his bird, who alights on a nearby tree limb where his keen eyesight can detect the slightest movement. Meanwhile, the falconer and his hunting party spread out, make noise, and disturb the ground cover in hopes of inducing squirrels to break their cover and scamper

When the squirrel finally "blinks" and begins to run, the hawk opens his throttle and dives, rolls, banks, and climbs through tree limbs like a *Top Gun* pilot. The squirrel soon tires of being chased and bails out of the tree into the waiting talons of the hawk. The falconer then quickly moves to the kill site to protect his bird and bag the squirrel after giving the bird a morsel of meat, which he carries in a small pouch belted around his waist.

In medieval times in older countries, when falconry was young, this method of hunting was quite effective. Few archers could bring down a game bird on the wing, guns were not yet invented, and trapping tools were crude and marginally productive.

Though small game hunting tools and techniques have undergone massive change over the centuries, falconry still thrives and probably always will because of the close bond that connects the falconer with his hawk.

Hunters of all types love the challenge and the chase, and hunting small game with birds of prey provides ample quantities of both.

Ken Cook

TREEING SQUIRRELS WITH BOB AND MOE

Like most youngsters growing up in the rural south, we cut our teeth, so to speak, hunting rabbits, squirrels, and quail. Not only was hunting small game enjoyable, but it also put meat on the family table and added variety to our weekly supper menu. My mother could make a squirrel and dumpling dish that was absolutely heavenly.

Though my hunting interests shifted to other game over the passing years, I never lost my love for squirrel hunting. And it mattered not whether we hunted with squirrel dogs or still-hunted along an oak tree ridge or flat.

When I heard about a kindred spirit with a good squirrel dog in Fannin County, Georgia, I jumped at the chance to hunt with Bob. Deer season was over, and we had the woods to ourselves. Now, Bob and Moe, his squirrel dog, are no pikers when it comes to squirrel hunting. This duo was the subject of an article in *Georgia Outdoor News* a while back.

Moe is a natural, short-tailed mountain cur, about fourteen years old, given to Bob about seven years ago. In the squirrel woods, this black-and-tan colored dog and his master are inseparable and nothing short of a squirrel-hunting machine. They know all the tricks that bushy tails play on hunters to escape detection.

When I arrived at Bob's shop, it was late in squirrel-time. Nine thirty is long past the hours when squirrels emerge from their nests and tree hollows to forage for fallen acorns. My travel time from Athens to Bob's house was slowed to a crawl by heavy fog in the mountains. Still, Bob was pretty sure we could find one or two.

Moe employs some unusual tactics when he hunts for squirrels. He "winds" them rather than tracking their scent on the ground. "When he trees a squirrel, he's always looking up the tree, and that's what I like about him," Bob said. "Moe never barks until he trees; and when he smells one, he gives a different bark than he does when he locates the squirrel. It's his way of telling me, 'Don't mess with me until I tree him,'" Bob added.

Squirrels are crafty when it comes to escaping detection. They like to flatten themselves against a limb or scrunch down in a fork, moving only when the hunter moves to the opposite side of the tree. That's why Moe always positions himself on the opposite side of the tree from Bob.

When detecting a treed squirrel becomes too difficult, Bob will break off a sizable tree limb and rub it vigorously against the tree trunk. Almost always, the squirrel will move and set himself up for the shot.

Bob's firearm of choice is a scoped, .17 caliber HMR bolt action rifle because it makes clean, instant kills and preserves the integrity of the meat.

In the course of our short, two-hour hunt, Moe treed about four squirrels, three of which our weak eyes couldn't locate, and one of which succumbed to Bob's sure aim. My time with Bob and Moe was special and nostalgic. It came as no surprise to learn that my guide was raised in a house on Squirrel Hunting Road.

Ken Cook

HUNTING MOUNTAIN BUSHY
TAILS IN THE SNOW

I overshot my turn-off and found myself on a one-lane, ice-caked road near the crest of Piedmont Mountain in Habersham County. Not a good place for a two-wheel-drive pickup, or any vehicle for that matter. Thanks to cell phones and good directions from my host, Mr. Edwards, I made it back to our rendezvous point and the start of a memorable squirrel hunt in the snow-covered Northeast Georgia mountains.

We had had to move our hunt date twice, and my anticipation was as high as a white oak tree. Despite the six to eight inches of snow that fell five days earlier, most of which still lingered, a chance to hunt squirrels with Mr. Edwards and his father and his famous pack of treeing feist dogs was not to be denied.

The elder Edwards, who retired from a local company, is a soft-spoken man with a long history of breeding and training treeing dogs. "My daddy bought me a ring-necked possum dog at a cow sale in 1951, and when that dog treed a possum, I thought I was on top of the world," he recalled. He soon moved into coonhounds and, for the next few decades, hunted coons, entered competitions, and filled his trophy cases. Only in the last three years, did he begin working with treeing feists and hunting squirrels.

Although there are similar treeing breeds, such as mountain and Kemmer feists, popular with squirrel hunters, treeing feists are the senior Edwards' first choice. He said these twenty-five to thirty pound feists are not only adept at treeing squirrels but because of their quickness, also make good dogs for coon, bear, hog, and western cougar hunting. "What impresses me about feists is their intelligence, ease of handling, and even temperament," he explained.

Meaning no disrespect to coon dogs, "I like to hunt with the dog and not hunt the dog," Edwards added. His top dog, Spanky, hunts by sight and scent. When a squirrel is treed, it often jumps or begins "timbering" from tree to tree. Spanky visually follows the squirrel's movements and ends up at the tree where the squirrel "settles."

Our first turnout was on a neighbor's property, and when the first squirrel of the day made its descent to the ground, the whole pack was on it in an instant, growling and scuffling for claiming rights. Mr. Edwards' son demonstrated his unique game release by grabbing the squirrel's tail and simultaneously lifting the dog's docked tail. Dog releases squirrel every time.

A living testimony to Mr. Edwards' dog training skill is a 165-pound great Dane that has been trained to tree squirrels. The dog was a gift from his daughter who raises them. "If you work a dog 'light' instead of expecting instant results, and give him time to do what he wants to do, he'll eventually do whatever you ask him," Edwards explained.

If you're ever driving the mountain roads in Habersham County during small game season and see a stately figure in the distance, astride a snow-white mule, it's not an apparition. It's only the senior Edwards riding Snowflake and following his pack of treeing feists.

Ken Cook

Feral
HOGS

HOG HUNTING WITH DOGS IN
THE SATILLA RIVER SWAMP

By 7:30 each morning, Mr. Dixon and his hunting buddy, Mr. Boatright, had crisscrossed the sandy roads and marked at least four different tracks left by feeding hogs the night before. They knew the direction these hogs had traveled, their approximate weight, and which track warranted the first turnout of the bay dogs. This is precision, live-capture hunting of large boars in the 200 pound plus class by two men who revere the sport.

Shooting a wild hog with a rifle doesn't hold a candle to grabbing the back legs of a 250 pound boar hog, avoiding contact with razor sharp two-inch tusks, holding his neck down with your knee, and trussing his feet like a rodeo bull dogger. In the time it takes to do this, your partner has tied off the bay dogs, pried open the catch dog's vise-grip hold on the hog's ear, and kept a lookout for a hog that might be lurking behind palmettos with revenge on his mind.

This sport is not for the faint of heart or those lacking agility and strength. From bay to catch to tie, the process is fast, requires lightning quick decisions, and bears an element of real danger. The dogs will attest to the hazards, and they have battle scars to prove it.

I was along for the story and the photographs when an urgent call from Boatright on the CB radio sent Mr. Dixon and me speeding in their direction. The dogs had bayed a mixed group of hogs, numbering close to fifteen, in a clear-cut covered with waist-high grass. What met my ears was a sound I had never heard before. "Can you hear

Ken Cook

them rattling," he asked me. After the capture of three hogs was complete, I asked about rattling and learned it was an alarm grunt, uttered in staccato fashion and used to threaten predators. When the chorus reached a crescendo, chills ran down my back.

Popular thinking about wild hogs (those born and raised in the swamp) is that they are proliferating because they breed so frequently and bear so many young. While that is certainly true, there is also another reason. Wild hogs are extremely wary, feed at night, and have the strength, stamina, and speed to outsmart experienced bay dogs. When hunting pressure mounts, hogs will often relocate or abandon an area.

Equipped with GPS-tracking devices on the dogs' collars, Dixon watched one of his bay dogs on our hunt pursue two different hogs through five miles of river swamp at an average pace of four miles per hour. We also tracked a hog that swam the swollen Big Satilla and back again with bay dogs in pursuit. It is not uncommon for wild hogs to reach speeds of thirty-five miles per hour on open ground.

Although none of the six live-captured hogs on our hunt topped Mr. Dixon's personal best of 425 pounds and two-and-a-half tusks, I have a newfound respect for the sport and the adventuresome men who pursue it.

SUS SCROFA IS A DIRTY WORD

t's also the scientific name for feral, free-ranging hogs. And if you are a farmer growing corn, cotton, or peanuts, or you are a landowner trying to increase his deer, turkey, and quail populations, you are likely to call them other names I can't print in this column.

The fact remains that these clever, omnivorous, destructive, piglet-making ruffians seem to be getting the best of us. And in spite of what we're doing to control feral hogs, the situation doesn't seem to be improving very much or very fast.

Current methods of controlling free-ranging hogs involve hunting, shooting, trapping, and exclusion fencing but the basic problem is, regardless of method, hogs are breeding faster than we can take them out.

Experts say that unless about 60% of a given herd can be taken out each year, the herd size will increase to its original size in three years. Texas, for example, which has a hog population of several million, measured their harvest rate in 2010 and found only 29% of their herd was harvested that year. Who's winning?

Consider these grim statistics: Sows begin breeding at six to ten months of age and drop two litters of four to eight piglets every twelve to fifteen months. Gestation period is 115 days, and piglets start foraging for themselves in two weeks and are weaned in three months. The typical size of mature adult hogs is one to five hundred pounds; Further, a feral hog herd can double in size in one to two years if left unchecked.

Originally concentrated in the Southeastern states, the feral hog population has now spread to thirty-nine states and four Canadian provinces, and best estimates put the total hog population at between two and six million. Annual destruction of crops, wildlife, and property is said to be $1.5 billion.

Georgia officials acknowledge that free-ranging hogs are destructive to Georgia forests, farms, orchards, crops, and timber plantations, but only in the last two years has collective action (a research survey) been taken to study the problem, raise awareness, and form a coalition.

The Warnell School of Forestry and Natural Resources at the University of Georgia took the lead in managing the 2012 Wild Pig Survey and reporting the findings. The goals of the survey were to assess the extent of hog distribution, assess damage by pigs, and gather opinions of landowners. The Southwest Cooperative Extension District of Georgia (forty-one counties, of which Clinch is the largest in total acreage) was the geographical focal point of the survey.

Among the 471 usable survey responses, the average crop loss (or crop-related damage) was $12,646 per respondent. For landowners who suffered damage and losses to timber, food plots, and lease values, loss was reported at $5,381 per respondent. Extrapolate these averages to all forty-one counties, and the total pig damage exceeds $81,000,000 yearly in the southwest extension district alone.

The survey also revealed that respondents felt current controls were not highly effective and "that state and federal agencies should provide more assistance with wild pig control."

Implicit in this quotation is the need for assistance from agricultural agencies, wildlife management groups, and associations such as the Farm Bureau, Georgia Forestry Association, USDA, DNR/WRD, Georgia Cotton Commission, QDMA, and others with vested interests. Most of these entities contributed to funding the survey and the formation of a Southwest Georgia District Wild Pig Working Group.

To close with an old adage, "Let's put our [collective] shoulders to the wheel, boys, because the ox is in the ditch."

FERAL HOG ROUNDUP IN
WAYNE COUNTY

I f you awakened from a Rip Van Winkle-like sleep and found yourself at the Jaycee Fairgrounds Building in Jesup, Georgia, on February 18 and 19, you might have mistook the large crowd for swine buyers at a livestock auction. Although the porkers weren't brought in live, they still earned $7,000 in cash for several sellers (hunters).

The occasion was the first annual Hog Jam, Wayne Tourism's third, crowd-pleasing outdoor event and the first one built around a competition among feral hog hunters for weighing in the heaviest pigs. Until now, two catfish tournaments, one in May and one in August, dominated Wayne County's annual event menu.

Hog hunters were allowed to register in three categories. The field included twenty-eight, four-man dog hunting teams; forty-one gun hunters; and fourteen archers. Cash payouts went to the top three places in each category. Overall, 182 hunters took to the fields, woods, and swamps in search of feral swine, and 70% of the hunters came from outside Wayne County.

With the scales straining each time the button was activated, over 3,338 pounds of porkers were weighed in by the first three winners in each of the three categories. Contest rules allowed dog-hunting teams to weigh in two hogs, while gun and bow hunters could only weigh one.

The Hog Jam proved to be a spectator magnet, even more so than a bass tournament weigh-in. When a truck laden with pork drove under the scales, onlookers moved to the area like gnats to an open can of potted meat in July. Nor was Hog Jam a male-oriented event. Kids and families outnumbered individuals.

Wayne Tourism seems to have the magic touch when it comes to creating big-purse, competitive outdoor sports events built around their abundant natural resources. With Hog Jam, they now have three successful events—and something for both hunters and fishermen. However, the real winner of these events is the city of Jesup (and Wayne County) because big tourism dollars accrue to the local community from these activities.

What Wayne Tourism is really good at, is taking an event concept and making it bigger, more exciting, and more enticing to attend. Hog Jam could have been just a competitive hog hunt, but this group didn't stop there. They added a barbecue (pork, of course) cooking competition (with prizes) and two days of guided hog hunting for ten Wounded Warriors from Fort Stewart.

I have now witnessed a catfish tournament and the Hog Jam, and it takes more than a good idea to produce a successful event. It takes leadership, hard work, and dedication from many local volunteers.

Make your plans and room reservations now to attend the next Hog Jam. It will be bigger and better. Wayne Tourism will see to that.

Ken Cook

Panthers, Cougars,
AND OTHER ALIASES

FACT OR FICTION: ARE LONG TAILED CATS IN GEORGIA?

N o outdoor subject ignites more controversy and campfire storytelling than panthers (a.k.a., cougars, pumas, mountain lions, and catamounts). Tales of bears, alligators, snakes, and other toothy critters won't hold a candle to a panther sighting. Georgia's Wildlife Resources Division has long maintained that there is no established, breeding cougar population in the state. No one has ever come forth with real evidence in the form of a dead panther or clear pictorial evidence. Hunters, farmers, rural residents, and town folk who claim to have seen a panther take exception to this statement.

I agree with DNR biologists that most of the panther sightings reported to them turn out to be cases of mistaken identity. In low-light conditions, bobcats, raccoons, and feral cats can be easily mistaken for panthers. Where I do draw the line, however, is when veteran hunters talk about their panther sighting in explicit detail and fail to gain an ear. Personally, I have seen one in broad daylight in a Georgia river swamp and believe they do exist in very isolated areas of Georgia.

But facts are facts, and I should point out two confirmed cougar kills in Georgia. In Atkinson County in October of 1995, a now retired WRD wildlife ranger investigated the case of a deer hunter who shot a cougar at close range from a deer stand and transported the animal to another location where it was dumped. The shooter and three other men, who took body parts from the animal for souvenirs, were charged with serious violations of Georgia game laws.

According to the ranger, "This cougar may have traveled from places as far away as the Osceola Forest in Florida, up through the Okefenokee swamp and all connecting bays and swamps to where it was shot near Roundabout swamp in Atkinson." The ranger surmised, "It was a healthy, wild-born and -raised species, and though I don't have the exact weight, I could guess that it weighed between 150 and 175 pounds." Photos indicated the cougar was a large, adult animal with light tan coloration.

In November 2008 in Troup County, near West Point Lake, another deer hunter shot and killed a cougar from his elevated stand. A visual examination of the animal by DNR biologists concluded that the cougar had likely been raised in captivity and was released [or escaped] into the wild. Some months later, a DNR news release was issued that stated, "Genetic testing by the National Cancer Institute, Laboratory of Genomic Diversity, has indicated that the cougar shot by a hunter in Troup County came from the resident Southern Florida panther population."

Nothing in this essay is intended to alarm those who enjoy the outdoors. There is no need to bring your pets in at night or postpone your camping trip. Cougars are solitary animals that prefer secluded habitat, avoid human contact, and hunt mainly for deer and turkey. Although there is a legal hunting season on mountain lions in South Dakota, our Florida and Georgia cats are endangered and deserve protection.

John McCowen, a rural Ben Hill County resident, was one of the first who contacted me about his panther sighting.

"I was strolling along a fire break about a mile north of my property in the summer of 1992 when a cougar crossed my path about ten yards in front of me," John related. "We both stopped and looked at each other; then he moved on. It was dark colored and had what seemed like yellow eyes."

Six years later, in June of 1998, McCowen encountered a second panther not far from where another resident had reported seeing one. "I have a large cypress pond surrounded by thick brush and tall gallberry bushes on my property; a thirty-acre field planted in six-inch-high cotton separated the pond from Sturgeon Creek," John said. "I was watching deer come out of the swampy pond heading for the creek when a cougar crossed the field and entered the creek. I watched it for three minutes, and it was dark in color and had a long, curled tail," John remembered. The height of the cotton had given John a visual reference on size and height of the cat.

Christi Schirack, who lives north of Fitzgerald and admits she doesn't read outdoor stories, sent me an excellent description of her panther sighting five years ago. Christi was walking her Sheltie collie one morning when a cougar crossed about fifteen steps in front of them. "I have seen lynx [bobcat] many times, and I knew this was no lynx because its fur was light tan and sleek. Also this cat had none of the stripes across its tail that a lynx usually has; its tail was several times longer than a lynx," Christi related. "It [the cat] took no notice of me or my dog," she concluded.

Bruce Harper of Fitzgerald called and described a panther sighting on the Ocilla Highway (US 129) south of Lake Beatrice. He was driving to Ocilla in the daylight hours when a large, black panther with a long, curled

Ken Cook

tail ran across the highway next to the bridge over Willacoochee Creek. This is the second report of a sighting in the Willacoochee Creek drainage.

Alan Mixon, twenty-three, was deer hunting with his brother-in-law on the family farm in Irwin County. Reedy Creek runs through their farm, and the Alapaha River is only a five-minute drive from their house. Late one fall afternoon, the two hunters observed a panther step out of the woods into a peanut field and crouch down as if it were stalking prey. "We were several hundred yards away, but through our rifle scopes, we could make out a large, black-colored cat with a long, curled tail," Alan said.

In June of 2011, Alan said he was called outside their house to listen to loud screams and throaty growls coming from the woods near their house. "We couldn't see the animal making the screams but it was like nothing I ever heard before," Alan recalled. Bobcats also emit blood-curdling screams and could have been the source rather than a panther, but the distinctiveness of the growls made Alan think otherwise.

Dr. Wayne Maris e-mailed to tell me about his panther experience in Southwest Florida, an area that is home base to the state's remaining population of endangered Florida Panthers. During that time, he studied a female panther with cubs in captivity and acquired a sound knowledge of their characteristics. About twenty years ago, Wayne witnessed a panther cross a highway bridge between Irwinville and Tifton. Two years ago, Wayne and his wife, Margie, both saw a large, tawny-colored animal with a long, sweeping tail cross the highway in front of them. It was midday near Thomson, Georgia.

Tammy Sewell, who in 2004 lived in Irwin County about a quarter mile from the Satilla River headwaters, sent me the first account of a possible panther attacking livestock on her father's farm. A young colt on the farm had been attacked by a predator and had gashes deep enough to require a veterinarian to close.

Not long after, as she was driving her daughter to school, Tammy spotted a large black animal near a bridge and, at first, mistook it for a big dog. As she drove closer, she described a black panther with a long, sweeping tail. "He sauntered across the road in no particular hurry even though I was stopped in the middle of the road. He [the panther] turned and looked at us and just kept walking," according to Tammy.

With suspicions now raised and pointing toward a panther as the culprit of the livestock attacks, the Sewells stayed on alert and took extra caution in watching their horses. Two more attacks occurred over a two-year period, one of which left bite marks and claw marks on one of the horses and a bloody gash on another. It was not until they turned two donkeys in with the horses did the mayhem stop, and only after one apparent bloody confrontation between donkey and predator. "We have seen this panther or his offspring at least four times in the past five years," Tammy said.

Jacob Littrell is a young man from the North Georgia mountains in Rabun County. A carpenter by trade, his father built their home by hand near the Tallulah River. The two Littrell boys grew up in the forests, hunting, fishing, and camping. Jacob related a story of sighting a panther sitting on a large boulder overlooking Lake Burton near the point where the Tallulah River flows into the lake. The sighting was in full afternoon daylight about two years ago. Jacob said he has seen a panther on this same boulder once since that time.

Not long after one of my panther columns was published, I ran into Julian Yarbrough at a local Fitzgerald restaurant. Julian told me that he once saw a female panther with cubs near Deep Creek, which I believe crosses under Georgia 107 two miles west of the Alapaha River. The time frame of his sighting was somehow lost in further conversation.

My last communication came in the form of a letter from a gentleman who asked that his name remain anonymous. Even though he had never seen a panther, he enjoyed my columns and shared an interest in reading more about these animals. The gentleman took the time to attach photocopies of two articles on Florida panthers, one from the *Atlanta Journal Constitution* and a second from the *Albany Herald* dating to 1994.

The anonymous writer said that he has a friend who did see a panther in 2007 along Hat Creek between Turner and Tift counties. The person was hunting deer at the time from an elevated tree stand. In closing, the writer debunked the existence of "black panthers." I had earlier reported seeing a black panther when hunting turkey in the Ocmulgee WMA several years ago.

My response to his challenge is that many color abnormalities exist in nature due to genetics and habitat. Otherwise, there would not be albino deer, piebald deer, and albino wild turkeys. These abnormal color variations are called melanistic specimens. Though the color standard for panthers, cougars, and mountain lions is variations of tan, a dark to black colored one just might be lurking somewhere in the South Georgia swamps.

Epilogue:

LAGNIAPPE

Wild Country

Previously
UNPUBLISHED

THE CHURCH OF THE GREAT OUTDOORS

I went to the Church of the Great Outdoors this morning. Reverently, I stepped inside the portal onto a platform where peace, beauty, and promise abound.

The cool early morning sunlight gently illuminated the longleaf pine needles and dark green foliage of the pecan trees.

At first, there were few sounds of nature but they grew in number and volume. A gaggle of squawking crows broke the silence; unseen roosters announced their whereabouts in the usual way; songbirds joined the chorus; a flock of honking Canada geese left their roosting pond for the short trip to food; and a lone woodpecker started the day with his staccato drumming on a tree.

A honeybee alights on the table in front of me. He has a purpose, though I know not what it is. A donkey emits a string of brays, perhaps to exercise his vocal chords but more likely to announce the presence of danger as a coyote trots along a nearby wood line.

God was delivering another perfect day at 131 Okeechobee Road. And all was well.

Though I cannot see him, the Holy Ghost is surely in this green tabernacle, walking between the evenly planted rows of slash and longleaf pine and pausing to show his pleasure with the surroundings and sounds of his creation.

The biscuit crumb I dropped among the trail of ants has been found, and like the bread of his body, was taken and eaten with reverence and gratitude.

A soft wisp of wind swirled through the wind chime pipes and produced a faint string of musical notes that no man nor instrument could duplicate.

The pecan trees in the yard are laden with fruit this year, and squirrels are anticipating an abundant harvest in November and full bellies over the winter.

Drought and summer heat told the canning pears, grapes, and scuppernongs to rest this year, conserve their energy, and skip the stress of fruit production.

Like a master orchestra conductor, God manages the seasons, cycles, and outputs from his creations.

A beautiful yellow swallow-tailed butterfly silently danced around the back porch, and cicadas signaled the close of the morning worship service.

With the sun now full in the eastern sky, all of God's creature are well into their daily routines. It has been an inspirational service this morning in the Church of the Great Outdoors. Praise the Lord.

BEYOND THE KILL

A diaphanous ground fog shrouded the gnarled, moss-draped limbs in the live oak hammock where Boone Barton sat in silence, patiently awaiting the sounds of early morning songbirds and raspy call of a crow. These birds were not his quarry. Nature had appointed them sentinels to announce the arrival of first light and to elicit the cacophonous gobble of a wild turkey.

Boone shifted his back against the live oak trunk, lowered the brim of his camouflage hat, and adjusted the palmetto fronds staked in the moist earth in front of him, standard protocol to conceal his outline and position. Soon, he hoped, he would be matching skills with a wary old Osceola gobbler.

Adjusting his amber eyeglasses in hopes of visually penetrating a slowly dissipating mist, Boone barely made out the outline of a cow pasture that lay before him. A well-seasoned woodsman and experienced turkey hunter, Boone surveyed the 180-degree stage in front of him, making mental notes of subtle landmarks, terrain shifts, and their distances from where he sat. Near the end of his visual survey, he heard the gobble of a turkey from another oak hammock across the pasture. Though his hearing was now diminished from years of shooting, Boone judged the distance to be about 150 yards from his setup.

Unchanged from his first turkey hunt fifty years ago, Boone's sensory responses were replicated as he felt his blood pressure rising and his breathing increase. He raised his ancient old Fox double gun to his knee and ever so slowly retrieved his beat up Lynch box call from the pocket of his hunting vest. Boone stroked the call with the precision of a first chair violinist deftly drawing his bow across a Stradivarius, emitting a crisp but barely audible sound. The old longbeard answered with a second gobble.

With the turkey still in his roost tree, Boone knew he had time to mentally identify all the approach options the turkey might take to make his way to the "hen." He also acknowledged that gobblers never do what you expect them to do, and their natural expectation is for the hen to come to them. With Boone's survey complete and his optimism as high as the pile of round hay bales he drove by on his way to the pasture, the muffled sound of wing beats reached his ears and he saw the gobbler sail effortlessly into the pasture. Another gobble tumbled from the beak of the bird as his long toes made contact with the pasture grass.

Like a chess player, a turkey hunter is never sure of his opponent's next move or how much time will elapse before it occurs. Visions often portray the turkey sprinting to the hidden hunter and committing ritualistic suicide. In other dreams, the gobbler, with inflated plumage and elegant dance steps, remains just beyond shotgun range and torments the hunter to the brink of madness. And sometimes, the gobbler just seems to lose interest and drift away into the forest cover. Boone was not at all sure what this old gobbler had in store for him.

Once on the ground, the old gobbler began a series of stop and go baby steps in Boone's direction, pausing frequently to stretch his neck and periscope his head to scan for danger. When he was assured an advance was safe, the turkey resumed his measured and calculated steps, each time bringing him closer to Boone. Now, sixty yards away, with the sunlight highlighting the bronze iridescent color on his breast feathers, the tom made a ninety-degree turn to the left and began moving toward the hammock to Boone's right. Within minutes, the turkey had disappeared into the trees, pausing to gobble one last time.

Boone surmised that the gobbler would try an old tactic of circling and approaching him from the side or behind. If he was correct, the conclusion of this hunt was most likely at hand. After an interminable period of time, Boone chose to execute a desperate maneuver, a move turkey hunters are cautioned never to do when a gobbler has already committed himself. Boone badly needed to know the turkey's current position, and a gobble would provide that proof. With trembling hands, Boone reached for his box call and began loud and aggressive "cutting." A thunderous gobble, less than forty yards away, reverberated through the cabbage palms and trampled the end of Boone's calling sequence.

A slowly unfolding encounter with an approaching wild turkey exacts a heavy toll on an aging hunter. Minutes are mistaken for hours by the human body. Lactic acid accumulates in the muscles, and they scream for relief; arms and legs follow the path of Rip Van Winkle, buttocks searching vain for a comfort zone. At close range, with a woods-smart old turkey, bodily movement is instant default. Boone acquiesced to the pain, took a deep breath, and steadied his body, even though the advantage had shifted and the odds of winning this match were slipping from his grasp. He could now only wait and hope.

In turkey hunting parlance, "spitting and drumming" is a term used to describe the close proximity of a turkey to a hunter. Drumming is thought to be a nonverbal sound made by rapid shaking of the turkey's feathers. Spitting is most likely a verbal sound emitted prior to the drumming motion. In any language, the sound is a hunter's worst nightmare or his best opportunity for a kill shot. Deciding against any movement, Boone sat motionless and simply digested the turkey's sounds until they drifted from earshot. With a smile on his face, he arose from his setup, gathered his gear, and began the short walk to his old IH Scout parked outside the cattle gap.

*

"Hey, Grandpa, did you get a turkey this morning," yelled a wiry, wide-eyed youngster as he ran toward the white Scout pulling into the driveway. "No, son, not this morning, but I had a heck of a hunt," Boone responded, still wearing a satisfied grin on his face. "Join me for a glass of sweet tea, and I'll tell you the story," he added.

Two empty tea tumblers sat on the dinette table as Boone finished his story. The youngster's eyes were wide open and riveted on his grandfather, now physically spent from the hunt and its replay. "Grandpa, when are you going to take me turkey hunting?" asked Jay, his grandson and soon-to-be hunting partner. You said I could go with you when I was twelve, and my birthday was two months ago," the youngster added. "I haven't shot my new Remington yet," he begged. "Well, son, we'll go next weekend, but you have to promise to do everything I tell you," Boone said with a stern tone in his voice.

*

Boone's vintage hunting vehicle bumped along the two-path road, occasionally jostling its occupants, who sat silently in their seats and stared blankly into the moonless night that lay beyond the truck's headlamps. Boone was

Ken Cook

an old-school grad fiercely loyal to his hunting truck, his turkey gun, and box call. Though his 1970 IH Scout bore scars from negotiating unforgiving muddy forest roads, the duct-taped tears on the seats were merely vestiges of memorable days afield.

Glassy-eyed and droopy-headed, Jay was already displaying telltale symptoms of sleep deprivation from his four in the morning wake-up call. This was a bad sign, thought Boone, who knew the situation would only worsen as the morning hours unfolded. Darkness abruptly enveloped them as Boone pulled the Scout off the road and extinguished the lights.

Although well endowed to hunt his magnificent game bird successfully, beginning hunters seldom become proficient at the sport in their early years of hunting. It is infinitely easier and faster to learn deer or dove hunting. There are so many ways to spook a tom without even recognizing which mistake was committed. Boone's hope, as the two softly made their way to a live oak hammock, was that Jay would at least return home having heard and seen wild turkeys.

Jay followed his grandfather well into the hammock's interior and stopped under a large oak broad enough for both to sit comfortably and within shotgun range of a dim but well-used game trail. Boone began cutting palmetto fronds and staking them in a semicircle around their setup. He knew turkeys roosted in the trees surrounding them and often used the trail to travel between roosting sites and feeding areas. Boone placed a hen decoy on the edge of the trail and returned to the oak to take his position next to Jay.

Soon, gobbling and hen talk broke the silence and reverberated through the hammock. Boone glanced down at his grandson, whose eyes were as wide as teacups. "I hear them, Grandpa," Jay whispered. An hour later, with no brown forms in view, Jay began to move his legs, rotate his head, and brush away an adventurous wolf spider that had crawled onto his pant leg. Boone reached down and squeezed the boy's arm. "Don't move, I think they're coming," he said quietly as he made three soft hen yelps on his call.

Through the thin openings of the palmetto spines, Jay saw three hens and a juvenile bird approach the decoy. Unaware, as yet, of human presence, the sounds of contented clucks and purrs enveloped the assemblage. "Raise your gun up son, but do it slowly and only when birds aren't staring at you; a gobbler should be right behind them," Boone whispered.

Before the hens completed their inspection of the rigid intruder, a thunderous gobble rang out and both hunters simultaneously glimpsed the tip of a gobbler's tail feathers over the top of their blind. As if a beauty pageant contestant starting a runway walk, the gobbler strutted toward the hens, wing tips drawing lines in the sand, feathers extended to exaggerate his size, and stopping occasionally to pirouette and show his best profile. It was a performance that Jay had never seen, and for a brief time, lured his attention from the gentle swaying of his shotgun barrel. The movement, however, did not escape the laser-like eyes of one of the hens.

Putt! Putt! Putt! The alarm bell rang loudly, and the most magnificent of nature shows was over, turkeys running and flying in all directions. Jay lowered his gun and looked up at his grandpa, utter disappointment, and surprise smeared from ear to ear. "Jay, we were busted, as they say in turkey hunting," Boone uttered, with a matter of fact response intended to let Jay off the hook. "Turkeys live every day of their lives in utter fear of predators, and as you just witnessed, they miss nothing," Boone added reassuringly as he gathered up their gear. As they walked out of the hammock, Boone turned and said, "You learned a valuable lesson today, son."

On the drive back to town, the irregular beats of the truck's engine muffled the light conversation in the cab but not the thoughts of Jay or Boone. Jay's blonde hair covered his eyes, and his chin rested on his chest. Boone knew Jay was crestfallen and sensed it was time for the best Lombardi halftime locker room talk he could muster.

"Son, you won't realize it 'til you're my age, but you were baptized this morning in the turkey woods. You see, turkey hunting ain't really about killing, although you will take your fair share in the years ahead; it's really about the experience. It's about going out with those you care about and want to be with, watching the sunrise, listening to the birds, and being on the front row of nature's grandest show. It's about the memories of hunts you tuck away in your mind and never forget, and the satisfaction that comes from telling turkey stories around the campfire. That's what turkey hunting is really about. So chalk this one up to experience, a disappointing first try, I admit, but stick with it. The true rewards are just over the crowns of those live oaks you see there in the distance."

About the
AUTHOR

KEN COOK

Born on a small farm in Southern Mississippi in 1941, Ken Cook knew chores came first before he could steal away for cane pole fishing or squirrel and rabbit hunting. As his family later moved to South Alabama and Georgia, he never lost his love of the outdoors or a thirst for adventure. Ken completed three marathons before age forty-one; earned a Royal Slam in turkey hunting; caught tarpon and sailfish in Florida and Costa Rica; took two horseback trips in Nevada and Canada; and canoed white-water rivers and guided his kids on an eighty-five-mile river trip. Ken is a lover of wing shooting, wild turkey hunting, and fishing for bass and panfish.

Ken Cook has won numerous awards for his newspaper writing, including the 2015 Pinnacle Award in Newspaper writing from the Professional Outdoor Media Association and Mossy Oak and a 2015 Outdoor Achievement Award for newspaper writing for his article, "The Legacy of Milton N. Hopkins."